# THIS IS A BOOK ABOUT FEAR, POWER, LOVE—AND REALITY.
# YOURS!

**STEWART EMERY**
was Werner Erhard's chief collaborator at *est*. Stewart Emery founded his own human potential workshop, which is more supportive, more positive. The techniques he uses to train tens of thousands of people every year in Boston, New York, Los Angeles, and San Francisco will work for you.

If someone gave you
**THE OWNER'S MANUAL FOR YOUR LIFE**
when you were born,
just imagine how much better off
you'd be now!

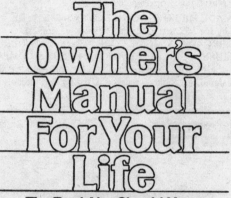

# The Owner's Manual For Your Life

## The Book You Should Have Gotten at Birth But Didn't

# Stewart Emery

PUBLISHED BY POCKET BOOKS NEW YORK

*To my friend and son Paul Emery*

Grateful acknowledgment is made to the following for permission to reprint their copyrighted material.

YOU MADE ME LOVE YOU (I Didn't Want To Do It)
Words by Joe McCarthy. Music by James V. Monaco.
© 1913 BROADWAY MUSIC CORP. © Renewed 1941 BROADWAY MUSIC CORP. and EDWIN H. MORRIS & COMPANY, A Division of MPL Communications, Inc. International Copyright Secured. All Rights Reserved. Used By Permission.

AS TIME GOES BY
Words, music by Herman Hupfeld.
© 1931 (Renewed) WARNER BROS. INC. All Rights Reserved. Used By Permission.

POCKET BOOKS, a division of Simon & Schuster, Inc.
1230 Avenue of the Americas, New York, N.Y. 10020

Published by arrangement with Doubleday & Company, Inc.
Library of Congress Catalog Card Number: 79-6862

ISBN: 0-671-46424-8

First Pocket Books printing March, 1984

10 9 8 7 6 5 4 3 2 1

POCKET and colophon are registered trademarks of Simon & Schuster, Inc.

Printed in the U.S.A.

# Contents

# POWER

## LOVE

# 1

# Introduction

This is a book about fear, power, and love. Within its pages we will learn how we have been preempted from ever knowing the experience of power and love that is our birthright as human beings by the mythology of fear and the impoverished models of reality we inherit at our birth.

If we have an impoverished model of reality we will lead an unhappy and impoverished life. If we have a rich model of reality, we will lead a rich and happy life. The purpose of this book is to show us how we can enrich our model of reality and be free from the past. It is the book we should have gotten at birth, but didn't.

## What Do We Mean by a "Model of Reality"?

A number of philosophers have pointed out that there is an irreducible difference between the world and our experience of it. We, as human beings, do not operate directly on the world and we do not each perceive reality in the same way. Through our primary senses of sight, hearing, touch, taste, and smell, and supported by our other modes of perception, we receive information about the world that we use to create our experience and a representation of the world in which we live.

Be clear that what we fashion is a representation of the world, but it is not, in fact, the world itself. We call a representation of something, which is not actually the thing itself, a model. In other words, we have all created a personal model of reality usually without ever recognizing that it is only a model and not reality itself.

We use the cause/effect relationship between our experience and our model of the world to generate our behavior. The personal model we have constructed of the world determines to a large degree what our experience will be in life and what choices we see available to us as we live in the world.

No two of us have exactly the same experiences and no two of us perceive the world in exactly the same way. It follows, then, that each of us will construct a slightly different representation of the world and live in a somewhat different personal reality.

Life is very rich and too often our experience is that it isn't. Our experience that it isn't is a consequence of our constructing a model of life which is not rich. The question is, why did we do this? The simple answer is fear, but this answer does not reveal the method by which we impoverish our model of reality and subsequently our life.

A series of constraints operate to ensure that the model we construct of reality is limited and does not contain all that there is. Consequently we live with an impoverished experience of being alive.

## Impoverishments Common to the Human Species

Our senses of sight, touch, taste, and smell are limited in their ability to provide us with information about the world around us. There are physical phenomena that lie outside the limits of these five accepted channels of sensory input. For example, sound waves below 20 cycles per second or above 20,000 cycles per second cannot be detected by human beings. Our dog will do much better in the high frequency department and therefore have a richer model of the reality we call sound.

The same is true about our ability to perceive what we call color. Our perception of color is dependent upon the different frequencies of vibration of the phenomenon we call light. Our perception of color shifts from what we call red at the low end of the spectrum to violet at the high end of the spectrum. Below our limit to perceive light visually, we can experience a vibration we call infrared, as heat. Above our limit to perceive light visually we can experience what we call ultraviolet light as a suntan. It is important for us to note that these physical phenomena of sound and light that lie outside our range of perception have exactly the same structure as the phenomena which lie within our range of perception.

We have developed the impoverishing habit of believing that if we cannot directly perceive a phenomenon, then the phenomenon does not exist. This is definitely a mistake.

It is not the purpose of this book to further examine this category of constraints that impoverish our model of the world. It is the purpose of this book to examine and discover ways of being free from two other categories of constraints, namely, cultural impoverishments and individual impoverishments.

## Cultural Impoverishments

A second way in which our model of the world differs from the world itself is as a result of a set of social constraints that filter the information we receive through our senses. Each culture constructs a model of social reality which implicitly defines what it means to be human. What it means to be human will therefore vary from culture to culture. The models of the culture are communicated through the language of the culture and generate the agreement by which the models are constructed and maintained. Individual members of a culture will not experience phenomena that cannot be described by the language. They will develop filters that eliminate such sensory input from being decoded and translated into experience.

I have personally witnessed people going through a personal transformation upon learning a foreign language, simply because the new language contains symbols that enable them to communicate and bring alive new experiences. I have a very dear friend who speaks Italian and French fluently in addition to English, which is her native language. When we travel in Europe together I enjoy watching her personality shift as she switches languages. When I pointed this out she asked, "Which one of me do you like the most?" I replied unhesitatingly, "The Italian version, for in this model of reality you are the most passionate and alive, and somehow your spirit seems more free."

Even within a given culture we find that the socially accepted model of reality will vary with the passage of time, to set up a series of conflicting ideals that become the neuroses of the culture. Throughout this book and particularly in the chapters devoted to sex, marriage, and romantic love, we will be exploring this phenomenon. We now come to the third set of constraints that are the basis for the most far-reaching differences among our experiences of being human and alive.

## Individual Impoverishments

Each of us has a set of individual constraints that in some way limit the richness of our personal model of reality. This process of impoverishment that is uniquely ours is based upon our own unique personal history. Each one of us has a set of experiences that become the building blocks of our personal history and are as unique to us as our fingerprints. In addition, each of us has a unique way of assembling these building blocks of experience into what becomes our personal model of reality. This unique way in which each of us constructs a model of the world will give rise to a set of interests, habits, likes, dislikes, emotional tendencies, and rules for behavior that are distinctly our own.

While we may argue that we have had little or no control over many of our experiences, it cannot be argued that we were forced to assemble these experiences in the way that we have, to produce the particular model of reality that is uniquely our own. I want you to imagine that each of our individual experiences is like a piece in a Tinker Toy construction set. When we get through building a model from all the pieces in our set of Tinker Toys, we can, if we don't like the result, pull the model apart and build one we do like.

The same principle holds true for our model of personal reality. Once we can recognize those aspects of it that are impoverished we can pull those segments of our model apart and reassemble the pieces to make an enriched model that then provides for an enriched experience of being alive.

It is not our past experiences that determine the quality of our life today, but rather it is *how we put them together*. This book will provide numerous insights into how we have put our experiences together, along with examples of how these experiences could be put together differently, thereby enriching our lives.

The purpose of all adventures in personal growth—whether recognized or not—is model enrichment. What we have to do to enrich our life is enrich our model of personal reality. What we have to do to enrich others' lives is to work with them as they reassemble their collection of experiences into a richer model of personal reality.

The specific mechanism by which we impoverish our model of the world can be divided into three broad categories. These are generalization, deletion, and distortion.

For example, a person who as a child was constantly rejected by his parents may make the *generalization* that he is not worth caring for. If later on in life someone tells him they love him he will not be able to hear it. He will *delete* and not receive all of the messages of caring. If these messages of caring are then drawn to his attention in such a way that he cannot ignore them he will, as likely as not, claim that the person offering the messages of caring has some selfish ulterior motive. He will, in this way, *distort*—in this case invalidate—these messages of caring.

In each of us, there is at work mechanisms of impoverishment that operate habitually in a pattern that is unique to us. We cannot break the habit of these patterns before we first become aware that we have them. This book will enable you to become aware that you have these mechanisms of impoverishment along with ways to be free of them.

The driving force behind our patterns of impoverishment is fear. How to manage our fear, then, is an important part of this book. So we will begin at the beginning, with fear.

# FEAR

## 2

## The Birth of Fear

### Life Is on the Other Side of Fear

If we ask, not "What is life?" but, more simply,
"When and where does life begin?" an answer
comes naturally:
"Life begins at birth."
Which seems so obvious it seems like a platitude.
But . . .
Within the womb, is the fetus dead?
Of course not.
Indeed, we know today that it enjoys all kinds of
sensations.
Even dreams!
And so no one, after serious reflection, can really
say that "life begins at birth."
What is it, then, that does begin at the moment we
are born?
What is it, if not life?
Fear!
Fear and the child are born together.
Fear is our faithful companion, our twin brother,
our shadow.
It will never let go its hold.
Until, remorselessly, it sees us into our grave.
—FREDERICK LEBOYER

I read the above passage for the first time in Stockholm while I was there to conduct an Actualizations Workshop. The statement that fear and the child are born together has traveled with me ever since. Fear is our human inheritance, the grim reaper of the experience of being alive.

## The Birth of Fear

To get a sense of the terrifying impact of our birth, take a few moments to consider what our life was like before we got born.

We lived in the absolute safety and comfort of our mother's womb. Unless we were a twin, it was a totally noncompetitive society. Our environment was warm and comfortable, we didn't have to struggle, work, or perform in any way at all in order to have our needs met. We didn't even have to be consciously aware of our needs or communicate them. Everything was anticipated and provided for. In retrospect these nine months of prenatal evolution will have been the most comfortable and safest time of our life. They will be regarded on some level in our subconscious mind as "the good old days."

## Goodbye Good Old Days

Then suddenly, for no good reason we know of, we find ourselves being forced down a passageway that is inherently too small, into a world we know nothing about. In other words, we get born. It's a matter of physiological fact that birth in the human being is a painful process; no other species experiences the level of discomfort during the birth process that a human being experiences. It is painful, distressing, and frightening for both the mother and the child.

Consider that from a perfectly supportive environment, we are suddenly thrust into a cold, brightly lit, noisy, and hostile world. The question must occur to us, "What have I done to deserve this?"

As our first experience of human contact, we are grabbed, held upside down, and whacked across the bottom. Then our life support systems are cut off, our eyes are syringed with a painful solution, and we have to breathe for the first time. We then get taken away from our mother and put in a room with a lot of other small babies, all screaming and crying as we are. There we lay, alone, with no certainty that our needs are going to be met. We have just been introduced to our lifelong companion, fear.

## The Hazards of Being Born a Person

So here we are, born into a world we don't understand. While we do, of course, have tremendous potential for understanding, none of our potential is actualized. None of our intelligence, none of our creative ability, none of our emotional capacity has yet been utilized or made real through action. So we immediately start putting our potential to work, attempting to understand the new environment in which we find ourselves.

We eventually get taken out of the maternity ward and brought home, where our mother does the best she knows how to put us in a comfortable environment. Of course, if there are visitors, we get put on display. I always feel that the scene of a baby being exhibited when visitors come round is reminiscent of the Bronx Zoo. Everybody's looking at us, examining us, prodding at us, poking us, hoping we will perform. If we do, everybody says the keeper did a great job, the keeper being our parents in this case.

More importantly, what really begins to shape our future life is what we go through when we are left alone, because as babies we become aware very quickly that our well-being is dependent upon external sources. We realize that our survival is dependent on things in the external environment, and that those things we need are made available to us by other people. It dawns on us that if we just lie happily in our crib, nobody takes any notice of us. Now this becomes a very counterproductive realization.

At this very early point in life we begin to get the message that just being ourselves is not enough. We've got to *do* something. Because if we just lie there being ourselves, our mother doesn't come to see us, and if we are left unnoticed and unattended for long enough, we will go through physical and emotional pain and eventually we'll die. So from our point of view as an infant, no attention for long enough equals death. (It appears to me, by the way, that this is the beginning of what becomes in most of us a tremendous need for attention.)

To more fully grasp the impact of this moment, imagine that you are a helpless infant, lying in your crib saying to yourself, "Now wait a minute. If I'm just lying here, nothing happens. If nothing happens for long enough, I start to have pains in my tummy; I start to get very wet and very smelly. In the womb, lying there was all I had to do. Therefore, in life, simply being here is not enough." And then you would most likely say to yourself, "If simply being here is not enough, what's enough? What will I have to do in life to get what I got automatically in the womb?"

Well, we come up with a brilliant one-word solution: *anything*. We will do anything that we think will work. Reaching this conclusion as an infant has a profound impact on the rest of our life. We'll talk more about this later.

### Oh No, It's You!

Let's consider another hazard of getting born. Obviously we have a much greater chance of getting picked up, cuddled, played with, and held warmly if we are really wanted by our parents. But as a matter of statistical probability, 50 percent of the people in this culture are here as a tribute to nothing more than their parents' carelessness in the area of birth control.

Mummy and Daddy's first reaction upon hearing about our conception may have been, "Oh shit!" And it's hard for us not to take that personally. Even though our parents may not overtly communicate that reaction to us, it gets communicated in other ways, through the nonverbal part of all communication. It's even possible that we received that kind of communication between our mother and our father in our prenatal state. So it may even be that some of our fears stared before we were born.

In any event, there exists the definite possibility that we were not wanted. If that's true, then as babies we have no way of knowing that we have been born into an impossible situation. In other words, even though we utilize all of our creativity and inherent love of life to produce the kind of caring, comforting, loving, playful communion with our parents that we are looking for, nothing we do works. And, of course, it's impossible under those circumstances not to conclude that there must be something the matter with *us*. We have no way of knowing that our parents' attitude toward us is a function of their inability to relate to our presence. We always see it as a function of our badness, or our wrongness, or our ugliness, or our awfulness.

At that point we can very easily just give up on ourselves and on life. And often, that's exactly what we do.

For example, I see women whose experience in childhood was clearly, "I was supposed to have been born a male." It can affect all their human interactions for the rest of their lives. They may even try to be male, and do all of the things that they think boys are supposed to do in an effort to get Daddy's attention or approval, or in an effort to make up for the fact that they had the audacity to be born a female.

So as we can see, one of the great hazards of being born is that we can be wrong on arrival. We pay an immedite price for this and, even worse, as we have no way of knowing that it truly isn't our fault, we construct an impoverished model of ourselves and life and thus impoverish the experience of the rest of our lives.

## Welcome Savior

Another hazard is that you may be born into a family where the relationship between your mother and father is very distressed. They may have planned to have you out of the belief that having a child would bring the marriage back together. Well, it's unfortunate when you arrive on the scene that nobody has taken the trouble to whisper in your ear that your mission, should you choose to accept it, is to save the marriage. You don't have any skills at marriage-saving. Besides, even in a well-established, healthy, creatively functioning marriage, the arrival of the first child is a trauma. It radically impacts upon the relationship. Now, suddenly, there are three, not two, and all the attention that formerly went to your father may now come to you.

So even in the best of marriages, a lot of adjustment is required to accommodate the new arrival. Patterns of living must change. Your parents' spontaneity is limited. They can't suddenly decide they want to go out for the evening. In addition, there are much greater demands on your mother's time than she may ever have known in her life. This will affect her capacity to relate to your father, who may not understand that. On some level, he may even begin to feel jealous, and not consciously recognize it. And all of this can happen even in a very good marriage.

The impact of your arrival on a troubled marriage can be catastrophic. The quality of the relationship between your parents may begin to further deteriorate with the arrival of you, the child. If you've been conceived with the expectation that you are to be a harbinger of joy and tranquility in a troubled marriage, you're already set up to be a disappointment. I mean, look at you. You are a living organism that takes away from your father the last little bit of attention that he ever got from your mother and you're the thing that screams and yells in the middle of the night when it looks like he's about to get lucky for the first time in nine months.

So, in your parents' eyes, you can be a tremendous disappointment—a failure. In some cases, the stress that your arrival places on the marriage may even be the straw that breaks the marriage's back. You may then carry the blame of one or both parents for causing the marriage to fail, which is their reaction to the expectations that you were going to cause it to succeed.

It is quite possible that you were born into a set of expectations people had of what you were going to do for them that were totally unrealistic. And this is the beginning of what, as we'll see later on, becomes perhaps the most debilitating fear of all: the fear that you are not enough, that you are inadequate and not worth caring for. Typically, you will develop this fear into a belief, into your operating model of reality.

The point is this: Most of us are, at the level of conscious thought, completely unaware of the circumstances of our birth, or of the powerful lifelong effects these events have on our ability to successfully live our lives. It may well have been that our parents were incapable of receiving the playful, joyful, curious, passionate interest in being alive that we brought with us as a newly born child. There's a chance that our parents in fact were very troubled people. When we really stop and consider, how often do we meet people who had parents who were talented and creative enough to have a relationship in which they nurtured each other, were playful with each other, were openly loving with each other, and felt supported by each other in their growth as individuals? Not very often.

## Summa Cum Lousy

Although we are the most highly educated people in history, there's an appalling lack of education in the area of how to relate successfully, and especially in the area of how to be a parent. We raise tomatoes more consciously than we raise children. As a matter of fact, to get a job on a farm today you are expected to have gone to college. So, to raise tomatoes you need a college degree. But the only qualification you need to be a parent is the ability to get laid one night. When we look at it that way, it's absolutely insane. First, it's crazy that it could even be that way; second, it's crazy that we let it be that way; and third, it's crazy because we don't even notice that it is that way.

It's quite possible that either or both our parents may have had their own psychological problems, emotional problems, or physiological problems, or had very low self-esteem. They most likely felt insecure about the fact that they actually had no idea how to raise a child.

As children it is unlikely that we could recognize that much of our pain was a product of our parents' difficulty in their own relationship and within themselves. As adults it is crucial that we recognize that we were not always the reason for or cause of these painful events.

## Forgive Them, They Know Not What They Do

I think it's important to establish here that we are not looking to pin the rap on anybody. This is not a matter of establishing blame. It's a matter of establishing the way that it was, and the impact that the way that it was has upon the way that it is and the way that it's going to be.

Often, when people see that the origins of their difficulties lie in their parental relationship, they blame their parents. But with parents, for our own emotional health, we've really got to say, "Forgive them, for they know not what they do." Our pain and developing fear are the wages of their innocent ignorance. They honestly do what they think is best, what they think is required of them as a loving parent. They don't know that it's a disaster. They really think that they're doing great. We know by our pain that it's awful, but in their reality they're doing a phenomenal job. No parent is deliberately bad.

## Give Me a Chance to Give

We have another very important need which we will be talking about in greater detail later, but it should be mentioned here. Our need is not just to receive from our parents; our need is to give and to be received *by* them. Obviously, we need to receive the components of our survival—food, clothing, shelter—but those are physiological components.

For us to become successful people we have self-esteem needs that must be met. The way self-esteem needs get met is by our being received; not by us receiving. Physiological survival is dependent upon physiological needs being met, but self-esteem is dependent upon us being received. And the part of us that we want received when we're a newly born child is our passionate curiosity, our inherent humor, laughter, joy, and love.

Somebody said once that children, poets, and great scientists have in common the ability to look at the world and be filled with wonder. And it's true. The fact of the matter is that the very qualities about us that are magical as children—the ability to wonder, to love, our passionate curiosity—all fade unless we are given the opportunity to contribute them to others.

Self-esteem accrues out of our ongoing experience

that who and what and the way we are makes a real and positive difference. If that's not forthcoming, even if all our other needs are met, even if we are given "love" as most people would think of love, we can grow up with no self-esteem at all.

Parents often don't understand this. "How come you don't love us?" they ask. "We've given you everything." And while the child can never verbalize it, inside he's really shrieking, "Yes, but you didn't ever let *me* give anything!"

## Mixed Messages Can Make You Crazy

As children, we seek ways to behave that secure for us the kind of attention and feedback we want, but the response we get from our parents can be very inconsistent. For example, when we're three or four years old we may have been given a sketch pad and a set of crayons or Magic Markers. Let's say that we play happily by ourselves in our nursery room, do simple little drawings that are totally free, unsuppressed, and creative, free of the restrictions that adults tend to have in their creative efforts. And we do these drawings that are absolutely wonderful.

Then let's say that Mom and Dad have visitors over for a dinner party, and we trot out our drawings. Everybody ohs and ahs, and tells us how wonderful they are. Mom and Dad are very excited because everybody is telling them how talented we are. They are proud of having perhaps given birth to another Picasso or Dali or some other creative, artistic genius. So they feel very validated. Soon the party's over, and our drawings are left taped up on the walls. The next afternoon Mommy puts us down to have a nap and decides she has to take a nap herself, because she's got a hangover from the night before.

But we're excited about what happened yesterday. We made our contribution, it was received and people were joyful, we could accept all the love and acknowledgment we got because we really experienced that we had done something to warrant it. We had our first little taste of what participation in life ought to be about, so we're very excited, too excited to sleep. We're lying in our crib saying, "Boy, yesterday was so good, I'd like some more of that. I know what I'll do, I'll do them some more drawings. When Mommy wakes up and Daddy gets home, I'll have a surprise for them, I'll have a whole new batch of drawings. And to save them the trouble of having to tape them up, I'll do them directly on the wall."

So we climb down the side of our crib, drag the kitchen stool across the living room, over to the wall, climb up on it, and proceed to do murals. Well, Daddy comes home from the office early because he's a little hung over too, and wants to spend some time with our mother, because he knows we'll be asleep. He walks in the front door, excited about seeing his wife, and instead, he sees us standing on the stool putting this mural on the wall with indelible markers. He goes crazy. He kicks the stool out from underneath us; we fall on the floor. He storms down the hall, kicks the bedroom door open, and in a loud voice demands to know how come that kid of hers is destroying the house that he's working overtime to pay for.

Meanwhile, we are lying in a crumpled heap on the floor, absolutely unable to understand what's happened to us. All we know is yesterday we were a hit, today we *are* hit.

We have no way of dealing with this kind of event, because we can't see that our behavior today is in any way different from our behavior yesterday. In fact, from our viewpoint, our behavior today is much better than our behavior yesterday. We saved paper, we saved sticky tape, and the drawings are bigger and even more creative. And what we get in the way of acknowledgment for our contribution and efforts is being physically or verbally beaten.

It's not that Mommy and Daddy are bad people. From their point of view, what we did was very upsetting. From our point of view, what we did was terrific and to us their reaction is an absolute shock. It's what we call a break in reality. Our expectations of what was going to happen are totally shattered. This kind of event has happened to each of us and can be intensely painful and damaging when we make an inappropriate generalization about life based upon our experience of a specific event.

## The Pivotal Event in Our Lives— the Beginning of Our End

If we have enough of these experiences, or enough of the experiences we spoke of earlier, where no matter what we do we don't get the sense of relationship or participation we are looking for from our parents, we eventually look at life and say, "You know what? It looks like life is a game in which I can't win."

That moment marks a pivot point in our lives. We have made an inappropriate generalization and once we've decided that we can't win, life becomes very different for us. Our decision that life is a game we can't win is an impoverishing generalization and marks the beginning of our end, the beginning of our gradual death. Along with the decision that we can't win comes the clear idea that we're not okay.

Given this model we have constructed of life, we proceed to collect what appears to us to be irrefutable evidence of our incompetence and wrongness as a person. If we look we will see that the evidence we amass is really a series of losses that become the elements of our fear. All fear is the fear of loss. There is not a fear you can think of that isn't a fear of loss.

Sometimes we think of it as "I fear pain," but it really is "I fear the loss of comfort." We think it's "I fear disapproval," but it's really "I fear the loss of the kind of relationship I have before I am disapproved of." What's really going on during all those early experiences is that we are being conditioned to be afraid of loss. So fear becomes the element of conditioning, and a specific fear is the fear of a specific loss. When we're a little baby lying in the crib, if we don't get attention, that represents a loss of ease or a loss of comfort. It is important to recognize that our fear is always our anticipation or expectation of loss.

As we have seen, our birth represents a tremendous loss to us: a loss of comfort, a loss of security, a loss from our point of view of automatically being nurtured, of automatically having our needs met. So we begin to perceive life as the thing that causes us loss. We begin to experience ourselves as victims in life, as victims in a series of events over which we have no control. We have modeled life as something to battle against. The thought that we could possibly ever win the battle against life becomes absolutely absent from our model. We may only model parts of life (e.g., relationships, or relationships with a specific sex) in this way, rather than all of life itself. The result will therefore be the impoverishment of those aspects of life to which we apply this model.

This is the point at which a shift takes place in our thinking, a pivotal shift that turns our life around 180 degrees. When we are born we're heading in the direction of life. But after we have a series of these events of pain or withdrawal of approval, from which we construct the generalization that we can't possibly win, we have turned ourselves around and become preoccupied with the avoidance of loss, and we are heading in the direction of death.

"The tragedy of life is not death, rather it is what we allow to die within us while we live," wrote Norman Cousins. So it is.

## How Do I Avoid Losing?

The problem in life now is: How do we avoid loss? We become motivated by the fear of loss, and once we have decided that what life is about is the avoidance of loss, the most we can get out of life is nothing.

We can demonstrate that mathematically. Let's assume that I have $10,000 in the bank, and I successfully guard it against loss for a year. What I have at the end of the year is $10,000. So what I got out of the year was nothing; on top of that, I'm down about 15 percent because of inflation. So once I've decided that the problem in life is the avoidance of loss, I've condemned myself to death through attrition. In other words, to turn around an old phrase, every day, in every way, I'm getting deader and deader and deader.

Once we become predominantly concerned with the avoidance of loss, we have entered into a state of decline.

The purpose of a book like this is to give us a chance to create another pivotal event—one that turns us back towards life.

I don't want to get dramatic about it in the theological sense as Martin Luther did, but, in a very real way, we are born doomed. Luther's model essentially claimed that the Earth was the province of the devil and not the province of God. He claimed that we arrived here doomed and didn't even have a chance to redeem ourselves before death. (Except for a few of us who were among the chosen and had been sent to Earth already redeemed by God, to do His work.) At best, the only consequence of our earthly tenure, according to Luther, was to make our doom no worse. There was nothing we could do to improve the fate awaiting us upon our death. I'd call that a slightly suppressive model, wouldn't you?

But in one sense Luther was correct. We do arrive here doomed. Not doomed by God, not condemned. God is not judgmental. (As we will see later in the book, that was a creative innovation, necessary for the Church's purposes.) But nonetheless, we are doomed by our inheritance of social constraint and suppressive models of life to construct our own impoverished model of reality built of generalizations and riddled with deletions. As a result, we suppress our experience of being alive.

We can even make a case for the fact that modern man is obsolete. We live in a world in which there is a phenomenal rate of change. Technologically, we have rolled a little snowball to the top of the hill, and now the thing's going downhill like an avalanche. We live in a world which is now beyond our capability to manage without the use of computers. The human brain is incapable of managing the world that it, by itself, was a catalyst for. The human brain made the little snowball and pushed it up to the top of the hill and over the crest. Now the snowball has grown bigger than the human brain can deal with. The modern world is reliant on the computer and will become even more so. In technical terms, we simply don't have enough inborn intelligence to manage the game that we have created.

It is incredibly dangerous to be operating in a world in which the rate of change has reached avalanche proportions with instincts that developed through a thousand centuries of insecurity—instincts that resist change. The explosion of technology in the last half century eclipses all technological change in recorded history. So what happens today in one week may have taken a thousand years to happen a long, long time ago.

This is not true about social change, and this is a very important distinction. The rate of social change, in fact, hasn't altered much throughout recorded history. As unstable as society may seem to be at this time, compared to the events of the Middle Ages, or to the decline and fall of the Roman Empire, it's business as usual.

People sometimes say, "Well, things really aren't changing any faster than usual." And they are not in the area of social change, because so far that has been a closed game. Socially, we swing from liberalism to conservatism in a cyclical fashion. But when we get to technological change, we're moving at an incredible rate, and this multiplies our fears. Our inability to deal with this rate of change, to process all the input, results in our feeling more and more alienated—more and more separated—more and more fearful.

Unless we recognize our condition we become the victim of the condition. Transformation is impossible until we consciously recognize that it is necessary. People will not set aside their old ways for the new until they personally see the need for it. As people, we know we are in pain, and we don't know the source of our pain. Worse, we think we know the source of it, and we are almost always wrong. All the input we've ever received is that our pain is caused externally. We pay a terrible price for our ignorance. It costs us the most valuable currency of all—our lives.

Unless we recognize the state of affairs we are in, unless we recognize the dangers we face, we will never change. Unless we know we are in the hole, we'll never get out.

I don't want you to say, "I am in the hole! My god, isn't that terrible?" If we get overwhelmed by the idea we are in the hole, we get further in the hole. So I don't want the idea that we're in the hole to be overwhelming; I want the recognition that we're in the hole to be received almost like it was a blessing. Because with the recognition that we're in the hole, we can say, "Oh, I better start climbing."

**3**

# On Loss and Our Solutions to Loss

Meanwhile, back at the game of us versus life, we had
decided that life was a game in which it was impossible
for us to win. This decision leads us to the next logical
question; to us the most important question of all—our
answer to which determines the quality of the rest of
our life. The question goes something like this: "If I
can't win, how can I avoid losing?"

As you read on, I invite you to look inside yourself
to see which of the following solutions you have
dramatized and employ on a regular basis. Not as a
condemnation of yourself or to find out how wrong
you are, but as a step in setting the stage for your own
liberation. Because in any area of your life that isn't
working, you will find, if you look, that you are
dramatizing a collection of solutions to the avoidance
of loss.

By the way, we are not saying there aren't times in
life when it's appropriate to be concerned with the
avoidance of loss. For example, car insurance is intelligent. What we are saying is that when the dominant
theme of our life becomes the avoidance of loss, life
for us is no longer a creative adventure: We have
sentenced ourselves to death.

### Don't Play

Here's the first and most obvious solution: *Don't
play*. The people who have decided that the solution to

life is *don't play* are the members of the living dead. We see their pale and frightened faces taking on color only when they consume excessive amounts of alcohol or drugs, or when they walk somewhere instead of driving their automobiles. They are closed and tragic figures.

Once the predominant theme of our life is *don't play*, we are on our way to death. The final and permanent version of this solution is, of course, suicide. It's interesting to note that people commit suicide in order to survive. I know that sounds like a contradiction in terms because traditionally we think of survival as a continuance of life. Survive (sur-vive) means to be on top of life. If you ask somebody how they are doing and they say, "I'm surviving," they usually look like life is on top of them. Survival in the context of the problem of "How do I avoid losing?" means "How do I avoid being at the effect of life, how do I avoid life being on top of me?" That's how people view survival. "How do I avoid losing with respect to life?" "How do I avoid being painfully the effect of life?" The answer may be, "I'll kill myself. And besides, if I do it right, I'll leave twenty guilty people behind."

## Quitting: the Grand Indulgence

Another solution is called "Quit the game before it's over." If we remember back to our childhood, we can recall times when we quit playing. Although we were called quitters, that was less painful than being faced with the fact that we were losers. As long as we quit before the game was over, we could hang on to the hope that perhaps we might have won, had we kept going. We'd give ourselves a few shades of possible victory that way.

Quitting has become the grand indulgence of our culture. I see America as a society preoccupied with the avoidance of loss. Therefore it's a culture in decline. I watch people quitting situations just too early to have learned the lessons that were there for them to learn. This is particularly true in our relationships and marriages.

Unfortunately, people don't think of life as an *art form*—as a movement from one lesson to another to another, until we gain mastery. The idea of mastery doesn't exist as a possibility in most people's minds; what exists instead is the preoccupation with the avoidance of loss. To turn that around, we have to begin to talk about life in terms of mastery and see each life situation as a lesson. We must always be asking: "What is the lesson, what did I learn today?"

As a people we are generally unwilling to step to the other side of our fear. We have become a culture of avoiders and quitters. We quit our job at the drop of a hat. We quit a relationship much too cheaply, motivated by the desire of avoidance. We quit doing anything the moment it becomes the least bit uncomfortable, frightening, or confusing. And this is tragic. Understand that I'm not advocating masochism either. But we do live in a disposable culture, a culture made up of the mentality of quitting. We dispose of the game, we dispose of the relationship, we dispose of the automobile, we dispose of everything. That adds to the climate of fear, because it further reinforces the notion that everything is temporal. It adds to our state of anxiety and breeds our neurosis.

People will quit in order to avoid being labeled as having lost. People would rather be quitters than losers.

## Well, I Wasn't Really Trying

Another solution that we may try which is similar to quitting is not to play 100 percent. I think we can all remember times as a child when we never really gave it our all.

That way if somebody said, "How come you didn't

win?" you can say, "Well, you know, I wasn't really trying." That breeds the half-hearted noncommittal mentality which is absolutely deadening.

## Destroy the Game

Another version of not really trying is: "It's a stupid game anyway." That solution is to *destroy the game*. The classic version of *destroy the game* you learned when you were a kid playing Monopoly. You remember. You were getting cleaned out, got up to get a cookie or go to the bathroom, and you just happen to knock the Monopoly board off the table onto the floor.

Not only children do this. Sitting across the aisle from me on an airplane during a recent flight from New York was a very chic couple. The woman was sitting next to the window, and they were playing backgammon, a game which could be considered the modern adult equivalent of Monopoly. We began to cross over the Rockies and there's fresh snow on the mountains—the first snow of the season. So she's turned around looking at that out the window. Suddenly there's a little bit of turbulence, not a lot. But I see his knee come up under the tray table, and wham, the backgammon game is airborne. She looks back at him and he says, "An air pocket." Suddenly he notices me smiling at him and he gets really embarrassed. So I give him a little victory sign, and he laughs. A little while later I notice a fresh beer has been delivered to my tray table. So I figure that the guy (for a cheat) at least has some class!

The other version of *destroy the game* is the one that is demonstrated by the *Dennis the Menace* comic strip in which Dennis and Margaret walk out the front door and Dennis says, "Hey that looks like Joey over there."

And Margaret, who is supercritical says, "Yeah, I wonder what he's up to this time."

Dennis says, "Let's find out. Hi, Joe, whatcha doing?"

Joey says, "I'm playing with my yo."

And Margaret says, in her critical voice, "You mean your yo-yo."

Joey says, "No, my yo-yo broke in half, and I'm playing with half of it, and that's a yo."

Dennis says, "Joey, that's great, how does it work?"

And Joey says, "Well, it goes down okay but it don't come up so good."

Margaret explodes in brutal criticism and exclaims: "Joey, that's ridiculous. You can't have fun playing with half of a yo-yo."

Joey is crushed and tears start to flow. Through his tears he responds, "Oh, I wish you had told me sooner, 'cause I just wasted a whole hour thinking I was having a good time."

We see this going on all the time. I watch the way we talk people out of having a good time with their yo (or anybody else's for that matter).

## If I Can't Win, Nobody Can

Another solution to the avoidance of loss is to *keep the game going forever.* If you can't destroy it, if you can't avoid playing, if you can't quit, then you keep it going forever. For me, the classic example of that came when I was counseling a married couple in their early fifties. They had been married in a very miserable relationship for thirty years. They were the kind of people who reminded me that there's no medical cure for bad vibes. They would come into the room and you could just feel the energy get oppressive. It was so bad, in fact, that I didn't work with the two of them together. I had to take one at a time. I started working with the husband and I said, "Do you have any sense of love for your wife?"

He said, "No."

I said, "Could you imagine that you could ever have any happiness with each other?"

He said, "No! We haven't had any happiness for so many years I can't imagine that I could ever be happy. Besides, marriage and life are supposed to be hard."

I said, "Are you even interested in trying?"

He said, "No!"

Obviously, not a very positive man. So I said, "Why don't you get a divorce, and let each other go?"

He said, "I'm not gonna let her go!"

"Why not?"

He said, "After all I put up with, you think I'm gonna risk letting her go free, and have her be happy with someone else while I'm left miserable by myself?"

I sat there stunned. She had similar feelings, by the way. It was as if they deserved each other. Their model was that if either of them were free and found happiness, then the other would thereby have lost. Neither one could conceive of finding happiness themselves. They were just preoccupied with the fear that the other might, which would have them as the loser. People will play the same absurd game with each other for a lifetime. In families, even after the parents die, the "surviving" children, conditioned to hold an impoverished model of life, will find a parental replacement to continue the deadening game.

What we need to recognize here is that there is this part of us that subconsciously, or even consciously for that matter, seeks to avoid losing. And not just on an intellectual level, but fundamentally on an emotional, feeling level. Notice that there is a part of us that experiences a sense of loss when we hear that somebody else has had a wonderful event happen to them. How many times when you hear somebody else's wonderful news, have you had that feeling, "Why not me?" I know people who are actors who feel a profound sense of loss whenever they hear of another actor getting a great part that they didn't even audition for. They use the event as an excuse to make an extra trip to the psychiatrist. The fact that the other actor may be their best friend doesn't help any. In fact, this may make it worse.

We need to recognize and catch that part of ourselves that operates in this way; recognize that every time we translate these feelings into action the action re-creates and perpetuates the feelings, giving them more and making them more real. Later we'll talk specifically about how we perpetuate our unwanted emotions and feelings.

## I Know, I'll Become the Game

Another solution to the avoidance of loss is this: Instead of playing the game, *be* the game which everybody else is playing. In other words, become what it is that other people are playing. Or become a symbol of the game. For example, you become the football, so you're not playing football, and everybody's playing you. The way in which we can become the football is to become a problem.

Consider the fact that you can get to be an instant somebody by killing someone who is somebody; by shooting John Lennon, or President Kennedy, or Martin Luther King. If you kill somebody like that, you not only get international media coverage, but the society will pay for you to be endlessly examined by a panel of psychiatrists.

You will get the undivided attention of professional do-gooders, and the public defender. You will get part of the media saying you can't be blamed because the society did it to you, and that was your way of dealing with the fact that the society did it to you.

And, of course, on the other hand, you will get all the attention of the people who want you put to death in the most painful and hideous way. So you are a football and two opposing teams are going for the end zones. The militants will want you in the end zone called "your execution." The liberals and the public defender will want you in the end zone called "you will be cared for by the state in some kind of comfort because, after all, you are insane and you cannot be held responsible, and you have to be taken care of."

In addition to all of this, if you choreograph it as brilliantly as Gary Gilmore did, you can get a million dollars up-front money for the media rights to this whole performance.

Consider another example. I was in New York ten days after the Son of Sam killer was apprehended. I'm in a magazine, tobacco, and paperback bookstore on Madison at Fifty-seventh, and I see they have two biographies of the Son of Sam on sale already. Within ten days! They must have had the books already typeset and were just waiting to get his name so they could drop it in all the blanks and run them off the press. They're selling at $4.95, and $5.95, and people are standing in line to buy them. Just try to get that kind of support for making a positive difference in our culture.

Of course, this has been true throughout recorded history. People who have tried to make a beneficial difference and advance beyond the limitations of what was already known, have been scoffed at, scorned and ridiculed. Galileo was set upon by the Grand Inquisitor.

Let us note in passing that the Inquisition left a trail of bloodshed of the relative order of magnitude of Hitler's holocaust. Furthermore, the means employed by the inquisitors during their suppressive reign of terror represented a blueprint for the atrocities of Hitler's Germany. All conducted by the Church and all in the name of God.

Fortunately for Galileo, set upon by the Grand Inquisitor for daring to suggest that the sun was the center of our system of planets (the Church maintained that the sun and other planets revolved around the earth), the influence of the powerful Medici family spared him the more unpleasant aspects of his antagonists' attention.

We can find any number of similar events in history, but suffice it to say that you will get a lot more attention for being a problem than you will for being a solution. If we listen to B. F. Skinner, we'll know that anything we give attention to, we will get more of, and anything we don't support, we will get less of. So we get what we support by giving it our attention. This is the principle of reinforcement at work. We support problems, we don't support solutions. Consequently we are creating a climate in which people who feel that their passage in life is a difficult one have actually been set up with a series of incentives to become a problem.

Look at your childhood: Remember the benefits of being sick? Becoming sick may have been the only way we could get treated like a person. Then we received special food, we were kept warm, we were cuddled, our mother and father temporarily restrained our brothers and sisters from beating us up. And if we timed it right, we missed the exams.

We have learned that there are tremendous benefits in being sick. To quote Norman Cousins from his book *Anatomy of an Illness:* "Physicians must resist the idea that technology will someday abolish disease. As long as humans feel threatened and helpless, they will seek the sanctuary that an illness provides."

I'm not advocating an inhuman approach to sickness, but I am saying we should recognize how much of human suffering is either consciously or subconsciously sought after. It is simply true that when we have experienced a profound sense of loss, or we feel particularly victimized, or feel just unable or unwilling to deal with the events that are coming down on us, we often get sick.

We go off to the doctor because it's his job to care for us. Just as we will go to a psychiatrist because it's his job to listen. One of the appeals of analysis is that for maybe the first time in our life someone will listen to us without interrupting.

Tragically, the systems of today say that if we don't get better, we can sue for malpractice. Then we get a fresh round of people who will give us a lot of attention—examining physicians, lawyers, a judge and a jury, and perhaps tens of thousands of dollars. That's a tremendous incentive to be irresponsible for our own life, it's a tremendous incentive to be unproductive, and a tremendous incentive not to master life. Examples of this scenario abound.

A few years back while conducting a workshop in Florida I was working with a woman who had a pain in her neck, dating from an auto accident seven years prior. I suspected that the pain lingered as a consequence of a mental and emotional need. As we worked together the pain disappeared.

Expecting the woman to be thrilled, I was dismayed to find instead that her first thoughts inquired: "How can I continue to collect insurance payments without the pain, and how can I make ends meet without the insurance payments?"

I am happy to relate that Emily was able to shift her viewpoint and recognize that the freedom from pain allowed an enrichment of her life far outweighing the temporary difficulties of the loss of insurance compensation.

The pain did not return.

Of course, there are people who genuinely do have accidents, or who are genuinely ill, and there are genuine cases of malpractice. But we can say with validity that illness is largely psychosomatic in its origin. Illness usually represents the satisfaction of a need.

We have created a tragic model of reality, one in which caring for one another has to be justified by our experiencing an extraordinary state of distress. This is a death-oriented outlook, and it's as absurd as it is sad.

## Another Way to Avoid Losing—Be Nice

Some of us never got past that tendency we talked about earlier of doing everything we could to please our parents. We ended up going through life trying to please everybody. Our way of avoiding losing is this: If we are nice enough, maybe nobody will tell us we actually lost, and they'll let us play anyway.

Have you ever noticed your own internal tendencies when in the presence of a person who's obviously operating out of the fear of loss, and who is protecting himself by playing nicey-nice? There's often a part of us that would like to take him out into the parking lot and beat him up. The way in which the nicey-nice doormat actually brings out the Genghis Khan in some of us demonstrates the principle of accountability. This is a very important principle which we will come back to a little later on.

## Here Comes the Judge

We live in a culture which for centuries has exalted the rational mind and asked of us that we make our emotions and feelings unimportant, that at all times we keep them under control. The result is that we no longer experience the fear of loss as an emotion or a feeling, and although we may have the physical symptoms of anxiety, we instead attempt to deal with loss as a concept. As a concept the fear of loss becomes, "I must not be wrong." The concept "I must not be wrong" is a rational component of the physical and emotional avoidance of loss. So we relentlessly struggle to avoid being wrong by demonstrating that everybody else is wrong, on the assumption that by default we get to be right if we are the least wrong.

As our solution to the avoidance of loss we play "here comes the judge." Of course, being the judge has tremendous benefits in our impoverished model of reality. We can't possibly ever be wrong.

We all know people who cannot tolerate being wrong—who are driven to prove that they are right *at any cost*. And always the cost is their life.

Once we have appointed ourselves as the judge, our greatest fear now becomes the fear of being judged by others. This is the fear that begins to run our lives. Consumed by the fear of being judged we struggle to avoid our fear by becoming even more judgmental of others. But the consequence is that our fear becomes even worse because, since we are judging everybody else, and are mentally putting them down, we automatically react to our (perhaps subconscious) assumption that everybody else is doing to us what we are doing to them. The principle of reinforcement is at work here.

### But It Isn't Finished Yet

Yet another way we can attempt to avoid losing is another version of "keep the game going forever." It's called *don't complete things*. If I come into your home and you are doing a painting, and I say, "That's a funny-looking painting," you can say, "But it isn't finished yet."

I know that we often feel a sense of apprehension when we are about to complete something. I remember an example from my own life. I am walking down Park Avenue in New York towards my publisher's office with the manuscript of my first book under my arm. It's a glorious day in New York. I should be elated, but I'm not. Instead I have this terrible sense of anxiety—of impending failure. Looking for the origin of my discomfort, I suddenly recognized that I am afraid that the New York *Times* literary critic was going to ridicule my book.

Well, as it happened, the reviewers of the New York *Times* did not ridicule the book, they simply ignored it.

The marketplace, however, did not ignore the book, so it has all turned out, but I still remember the fear.

I also remember this fear from childhood. How many drawings did we finish, only to have somebody say, "The sky isn't green, the sky is blue." Even if they don't attack it, they may do something we find even worse, ignore it.

So there's tremendous safety in not completing things. Procrastination is mostly about the fear of criticism—the fear of being wrong. This is also what laziness is about. People aren't lazy, they just don't want to be judged. In the presence of the fear of being wrong, we come up with the solution called laziness, or we come up with the solution called "don't complete it, leave it unfinished."

Once again, let us recognize that sometimes it is appropriate to protect ourselves in life because sometimes there are real threats. What is damaging to us, however, is that the attempt to protect ourselves from loss becomes our standard operating procedure. And we now do this automatically, without being consciously aware of it most of the time.

As we struggle to protect ourselves from loss in the presence of nonexistent threats, we become absolutely indiscriminate in the automatic application of our full repertoire of avoidance solutions. And worse, although they are all solutions to avoid a problem that in reality we do not have, using them will reinforce our belief that we do really have the problem.

To draw from my first book, being born is like waking up inside a dream and not knowing it. In our sleep we have amassed a garrison of devices and decisions to protect ourselves from the threat from outside. We seek to protect ourselves from all that we feel separate from. We have barricaded ourselves in our cabin to fight off the Indians while we wait in fervent hope for the cavalry to arrive and save us.

Well, I have good news and I have bad news. First, the bad news: The cavalry isn't coming. Sorry, but Rin Tin Tin, John Wayne, and the detachment from Fort Apache are not going to come riding over the hill. No one is going to save us from the Indians of our life.

When we really get the hopelessness of that fact, it may make us very sad. It will also allow us to get the good news. And the good news is, there aren't any Indians. There is only a universe that supports us in making life a joyful adventure or an endless nightmare. So while there is no hope, it is also true that there is no hope needed.

Successful living requires that we be creatively adventurous when the climate favors it, and only when the climate is indeed hostile should we take the prudent and necessary steps to protect ourselves.

# 4

# On the Hole We Are In and How to Get Out

At this point, I want to introduce an important principle—one that we will come back to very often in the course of our exploration together. This principle describes the mechanics behind the idea that each of us actually creates the circumstances of our lives, i.e., the reality of our accountability.

The principle can be stated this way: *The idea of feeling behind our behavior will be reinforced by the behavior itself.*

In other words, if we are motivated out of fear of loss, we will act in a way that in the long run will reinforce that fear and ultimately can cause the loss to actually come to pass, thereby justifying and reinforcing the fear.

For example, the way in which insecure people behave around other people guarantees that other people will relate to them in a nonaccepting way, i.e., that what they are afraid of will become a reality. If they are afraid of being rejected, they will act in a way that makes them very rejectable. We have an enormous, but unrecognized, ability to powerfully communmicate without ever opening our mouths. In fact, 60 to 70 percent of all communication is non-verbal.

We nonverbally communicate our fear of being rejected to other people who have their own level of fear of being rejected. Our nonverbal statement of fear makes them an offer they can't refuse. The fact that our fear is greater than theirs invites them to judge us, because, remember, they're playing "here comes the judge" as a solution. So they judge us to put us down in an attempt to elevate themselves. The result to us looks like rejection.

This seems to prove the fact that people are always going to judge us, which adds credibility to our fears, credibility to our viewpoint, credibility to our apprehensions that we are going to be judged and rejected. In this way, our impoverished model of reality is reinforced. In other words, we continually create our own insecurity.

Similar examples abound in many different areas of our life. They happen every day to each of us. We'll talk more about this later.

Everyone should know that we have to live according to our means. Economists have been telling us this for ages, and we refuse to listen. Our economy has for many years been based on a "buy now pay later" system. Well now, welcome to *later*.

That we can't live beyond our means applies to all areas of our life. We can't life beyond the means of our wisdom, our awareness, our skill, our evolution. Imagine that you or I are faced with a large family to feed, and that we have no money. Imagine that all we have in the pantry is one fish, one loaf of bread, and one glass of wine; given our means, that would be a problem for you and me. We would probably be anxious and begin to protect ourselves from loss, although it would be appropriate for us to look for ways to be creative and productive. If, however, we had the level of mastery of the man they call Jesus of Nazareth, having only one fish, one loaf of bread, and one glass of wine wouldn't be a problem. Because *he* managed to feed the multitudes.

Or imagine that our enemies are pursuing us and we have a river to cross, as in some of the old westerns, and we are experiencing a state of fear. We had better protect ourselves from loss, and also had better come up with some creative solutions. Now if we can do a number like the parting of the Red Sea, it would definitely take a lot of the threat out of life.

The more of living you master, the less of life you fear. This is a very important principle: The more of life you master, the less of life you fear.

Mastery is on the other side of our fear. We must go through our fear on our way to higher levels of mastery.

We need to recognize where we are. We need to be responsible about recognizing our own level of evolution. We must learn to operate within the budget of our wisdom, our mastery, our skill, our general level of awareness and consciousness.

Mastery can be defined as the ability to actualize. A high ability to actualize is mastery. That is our ultimate and only real security. The only way we can solve the problem of our insecurity is to experience that we possess a high level of ability to actualize. The only way we can experience a high ability to actualize is to do the work, learn the lessons, and acquire the life skills, as we travel to the other side of our fear.

Once we have decided that the problem in life is how to avoid loss, we have relinquished ownership of our own life. We don't hold title anymore, fear does.

Fritz Perls, the father of gestalt psychology, and often called a magician, always talked to people about owning their lives. Specifically, he would command people to own their emotions, to own their feelings, rather than to appropriate the cause of their emotions and their feelings outside of themselves. We are conditioned to think in terms of somebody making us angry, somebody making us sad, somebody upsetting us, somebody hurting our feelings. We have acquired the habit of seeking to blame others for our feelings. We have even been set up to blame other people for our good feelings. We have songs that say, "You Made Me Love You—I Didn't Want to Do It," which is absolute nonsense. We have songs like "It Had to Be You." No, it didn't, it did not have to be you.

The programming that we are given leads us to a point where we really believe that external circumstances and other people are the origins and the causes of our emotions and of our feelings and of our life. At this point we have no ownership at all. We are firmly established in the position of a victim. We see ourselves as the effect of life and are looking to avoid being the effect of life, to avoid the losses of life.

Once we begin operating out of this model, there isn't any good side. Here's what I mean: Freud pointed out that under the circumstances we've been describing people will seek to pursue pleasure and avoid pain. (Freud's observations and commentary on human nature appear to be accurate until we discover the vital exception: They apply accurately to 98 percent of the population, but not the 2 percent who are highly self-actualized. Highly self-actualized people are playing an entirely different game. More about this later.)

Let's look at this whole idea of the pursuit of pleasure. Let's say that we've had our pivotal traumatic experience. In other words, we have decided that life is a game we can't win; now all we can do is try and avoid losing. Consequently, every day in some way or other we are becoming deader and deader and deader. Maybe the best life ever gets for us is when it doesn't hurt. This is likely to be so if we are constantly preoccupied with the avoidance of pain and loss.

As we struggle to avoid the pain of loss and as we pursue pleasure, we are operating in a model that holds us as the effect of life. Thus, we perceive—inaccurately—that the experience of pleasure is also an effect. For example, we want to "fall in love." The very idea of falling is the idea of an effect. We don't have any ownership of our life when we are falling. When you are falling, gravity is in charge of your life. Or we can say that we are being "swept off our feet."

Now we encounter another critical principle: *Prolonged exposure to anything that we experience as an effect will result in our becoming numb to the effect.* We see that clearly in the case of drugs. If you take a drug in a constant dosage for any period of time, you build up an immunity, a resistance, a tolerance to the drug. Prolonged exposure to that which we are the effect of establishes tolerance.

Just as we build up a tolerance to drugs, we build up a tolerance to our pleasures. If we successfully pursue pleasure as an effect, our next drive, having pursued it and found it, is to possess it. The very possession of the pleasure which we have searched for, pursued, and found results in our building up a tolerance to the experience of the pleasure. The pleasure is no longer experienceable at its present level of intensity. So our very success at seeking, finding, and possessing what we believe we want sets us up for another experience of loss, simply because we build tolerance to the pleasure. Building tolerance to the pleasure is akin to losing it.

When we live as if we are the effect of life, both our

pain and our pleasure, everything has a ring of loss about it.

This is a condition that most people will never, ever be free of. We'll see later on why most relationships never survive the fact that the two people fell in love. People find a job they love and then one day they don't love it anymore. Love is replaced by boredom with agonizing regularity.

In this model, of course, the solution is always change. For a while it looks as though change is an answer, and that's what this culture is built upon. Change. Throw away one, you get another one. Changing fashions, changing cars, changing lovers, changing everything. But, we don't see that the addiction to change produces a tolerance to change. So we live in an overstimulated culture, and because we are overstimulated, our ability to experience any of the stimulants is eroded until we become finally incapable of experiencing anything.

When we get to the point where we become incapable of experiencing life, we have joined the ranks of the living dead. Because being alive is *the ability to experience*. Being alive is to be experiencing life; that's what being alive is about. But given the model we grew up in, that's the one thing we won't be able to do. So we become simply a portable brain. Our body degenerates into something that transports our brain around, and all that's left in life for us is disembodied mental activity. Which, of course, is what many of the philosophers told us we ought to be about.

On the eve of the hundredth anniversary of Albert Einstein's birth, I was talking to Robert Muller in the United Nations. This man was very close to U Thant, close to Dag Hammarskjöld, and today holds a number of posts at the UN. Robert Muller describes himself as an optimist by choice. He says that an optimist by choice is a person who has studied reality, come to peace with all the evidence that men are destructive and evil, and chooses instead a model of humanity contained in the lives of men and women whose goodness, beauty, and pursuit of truth represent the glorious exception that illuminates the darkness of fear and mediocrity.

Most people claim they are optimists as an avoidance of life. But then there are those rare, highly actualized people, like Robert Muller, who have looked at reality, who understand all the risks, and all the possible horrors and who are still optimistic about humanity. Here is a man who, after joining an active Resistance Maquis, survived being captured by the Nazis. He has seen a lot of the worst that the world has to offer.

We were talking about the problems confronting the world. We talked about the obvious ones—the energy crisis, the fact that we've plundered the world's resources and that the world now is signaling its inability to support our plunder forevermore. We talked about the oppression and fear that people live under, the material, emotional, physical, and political terror, suppression, and tyranny they suffer. But he went on to say something that really struck me. He said, "Stewart, perhaps the problem in the world out of which all of the others come is people's fundamental inability to experience happiness."

I did not expect to hear that expressed in the building that housed the secretariat of the United Nations, where people find little cause for optimism.

Robert Muller has written a wonderful book called *Most of All They Taught Me Happiness*. Obviously, he is a man who knows and lives with the experience happiness, though not quite sure how and why his experience is a rarity. He recognizes the importance of the experience of happiness, but he isn't certain he can tell somebody else what the structure of happiness is, with the result that they too will have the experience.

As someone who is committed to understanding and usefully transmitting the structure of happiness, I know that many people consider it indulgent to talk about being happy. But I'll tell you something: If we're not happy, we are in conflict, and if we are in conflict, we'll use the tools of conflict. And if we use the tools of conflict, we will destroy the world. *So happiness becomes not an indulgence, but an essential condition for the continuation of life as we know it on this Earth.*

Now where this is all leading us to is our brain. There's a lot of discussion today about the two hemispheres of the brain, the left and the right. The left hemisphere is connected to the right side of the body and for almost all people that represents the rational self: It functions sequentially, logically, deductively, rationally, linearly. It's the part of us that has to be right. It's the part of us that is always seeking to survive intellectually. That side of us is incapable of experiencing peace, satisfaction, love, happiness, or fulfillment. Yet, it's the side of us that the culture has favored; it's the side of us that built the culture that favors the side of us that built the culture that favors the side of us that built the culture. It's almost like the chicken and the egg. I don't know which came first— the left side of the brain or the culture that favors the left side of the brain.

On the other side is the right hemisphere of the brain, which is connected to the left side of the body. This is the part of us that is creative. It functions inductively, intuitively; it doesn't have to operate sequentially.

It's the right side of the brain that's capable of experiencing joy, peace, satisfaction, and a sense of completion. The left side of the brain experiences separation; the right side of the brain experiences relationship. So the experience of being happy is a right-brain experience.

A good way of illustrating the difference between the left side and the right side is this: Think about laughter. Laughter is a right hemisphere activity, because you can't get from where you are to laughter through the use of your rational mind, as you'll find out anytime anybody attempts to explain to you a joke you didn't get. Laughter is a right hemisphere experience. Laughter requires that kind of inferential leap, and the left hemisphere can only conclude, it can't infer. Happiness, laughter, the very experience we want in life resides on the right side of the brain, the side that doesn't get much support in our culture.

So the right side of the brain already is where the left side of the brain is trying to get the rest of us. Of course, we don't know that the left side is not capable of knowing that.

Let's look again at this model of life in which we are victims. In this model we have two choices of victimhood. In one we are a victim in a painful way. In another, we are a victim in a pleasurable way. We are seeking to avoid pain, which is being a victim in a painful way, and to pursue pleasure, in which case we become a victim in a pleasurable way. As long as we use this model of reality while we struggle to be alive, we will build tolerance to both our pain and our pleasure. In this impoverished model of reality the ultimate form of tolerance is death. While death is the ultimate solution to life given this model, first we try another solution; we seek the new and different.

This is the new, now, never-before society. Every advertisement says "New!" "For the First Time!" "Never Before," "New, Improved." It's set up to provide us with constant stimuli but, as we have seen, this builds our tolerance to the experience of being stimulated. The result is that we lose the ability to experience life and continue only to survive in the physiological sense, for in every other sense we have died.

Now, you might be saying, "Well, how are we going to dig ourselves out of that woodpile?" It looks hopeless. Because you can see that in a situation where you have a chance to avoid pain and pursue pleasure, you will pursue pleasure. But when pleasure is an event that you experience as an effect, you build tolerance, which costs you the loss of the pleasure returning you to the experience of pain and loss which you wanted to get away from in the first place.

In this way, we become like a rat on one of Professor Skinner's laboratory treadmills. When we are on this treadmill that is mistaken for life, death becomes, at least subconsciously, a very seductive opportunity. Life, for most people, eventually becomes what they are doing while they are waiting to die. Life becomes a waiting room: The appointment is with death.

The question is: What would it take to get out? *What will it take to get out?*

First off, what it will take to get out is to know that we're in. Hopefully, nobody can read these first few chapters without recognizing that, on some level, they're in. The next thing it would take to get out is to accept that getting out is necessary and possible. We are talking about making an escape *to* life, and giving up our attempts to escape *from* life. As previously noted, nobody will set aside his old ways for the new until he personally sees the need for it. So we've got to see personally the need for getting out and accept, if only on an experimental basis, that it is possible. This is step number one.

This is a message that Christ, Buddha, and other great teachers want us to receive: Out is possible. We may have trouble accepting that out is possible for us, but if we can hear even a part of their teachings, they offer us a new beginning. Unfortunately we usually create a separation between those who are fully alive and ourselves. We reason that if they're different, if they are not ordinary people as we are, then they are in a different game. If they are in a different game, or if they are not really human, then we didn't lose. This provides a way for us not to accept that we're dying in the prison of an impoverished model of reality.

A number of the great philosophers tried to establish that getting out of this prison is possible and that the escape route is the rational mind. This idea was resurrected and promoted by René Descartes in the seventeenth century. He kept saying that out was possible, and that the rational mind was the key. Well, out is possible, and you can't get there intellectually. Intellectually you can read about water, but getting wet has to be experienced, and the rational mind does not experience. It only thinks about experience; it only conceptualizes experience. It doesn't actually experience.

## Step Two: Make a Commitment

The next step in getting out is to make a commitment to getting out. Most people don't ever do that. Most people sit around wishing life would change. But it never does, not until we make a commitment to enriching our personal model of reality, knowing that we still may never get out. We are talking about making a commitment to the process of getting out. And our commitment to the process must be independent of whether or not we actually accomplish the task. Commitment to the process comes out of the pragmatic recognition that death for us is not a viable alternative. At this point we've got to see consciously that staying in our self-created hole is not a viable alternative.

So you say, "Okay, now I've got to make a commitment to getting out. But what does that look like? What does it mean?"

What that means is committing ourselves to becoming aware of the behavior, attitude, beliefs, and viewpoints that propel us down a path of death and dying. It means committing ourselves to shedding those beliefs, to shedding those attitudes, and to shedding those aspects of our behavior that represent a commitment to, and the pursuit of, death and dying. Most importantly, it means making a commitment to pursue those attitudes, beliefs, and ways of behaving that represent a commitment to life, to getting out, and this takes *discipline*.

Discipline for most of us is a dirty word. It involves us in work. That's another dirty word. Tragically, in response to this idea I often hear: "What, you want me to work? I'll transform if I can schedule it between playing tennis and getting laid. And if it leaves me enough money for a new set of high performance exhausts for my Porsche, or if I still have enough left over to buy a couple of grams of coke, then I'm interested."

## Viewing It Differently, Doing It Differently

What gets us out is viewing life with a different viewpoint and doing life with different behavior. At the risk of oversimplification, it could be said that Skinner tried to change the world by changing people's behavior, and Freud tried to change the world by explaining and changing people's viewpoints. But you won't ultimately transform your life unless you do both.

A lot of therapy doesn't demand altered behavior. Yet, on the other hand, to simply demand altered behavior doesn't work either. Because, you see, if our behavior and our viewpoint are inconsistent we will experience conflict.

Let's say we are in a situation where our life doesn't work because our behavior is unworkable. Our behavior is unworkable because our viewpoint is unworkable. We'll be unsuccessful in life because our viewpoint and our behavior come out of an impoverished, in-the-hole model of reality.

Let's say we do something—therapy, a seminar, anything—to enrich our model and change our viewpoint. Now we have a more workable, out-of-the-hole viewpoint. But, if we don't now display the behavior that is consistent with an out-of-the-hole viewpoint, we'll still be in the hole and we'll still experience conflict.

In addition to our experience of conflict, we will begin to drift back to our old attitudes, beliefs, and viewpoint, because the old behavioral habits will re-create our old unwanted emotions and feelings, and our old unwanted emotions and feelings will subconsciously demand the reinstatement of our old attitudes, beliefs, and viewpoint.

On the other hand, we can give ourselves workable, out-of-the-hole behavior through behavior modification, because behavior modification works. (But then so does torture, as somebody pointed out.) While we may modify our behavior, if we still have the same in-the-hole viewpoint, if we still have an impoverished model of reality, then we will still be in conflict, and we will still be in the hole.

Our viewpoint and our behavior must be consistent. It's like climbing a wall and having each leg on the rung of a different ladder. One ladder is called viewpoint and the other ladder is called behavior. To get out, we have to take a step at a time up each ladder.

## Viewpoint: The Power of Accountability

At this stage a good question would be, "What is a workable, out-of-the-hole viewpoint?" The out-of-the-hole viewpoint is one we call the viewpoint of accountability. The word *accountable* means "to stand and be counted, as a part or a cause or an agent or a source, of an event or set of circumstances." So a viewpoint of accountability means that we will now look at life from the point of view that we are a part of it rather than separate from it. That we are an agent for life rather than a victim of it. That we are a source of what happens to us and that we are able to cause worthwhile things to happen. The following true story illustrates the power of this viewpoint.

On the last day of a workshop in Hollywood, California, we were talking about accountability when a woman raised her hand and stood up. "I want to tell my story," she said.

The story began to unfold. She and the friend with whom she was staying had gone home on Thursday night, the first night of the workshop. There they were held at gunpoint, then robbed and raped.

Everybody, of course, gasped, "How terrible!"

She replied, "No, I don't want you to see it that way," and continued, "The person I was with was very frightened and was tending towards hysteria. But I've been doing a lot of work on myself and I understand about this viewpoint of accountability. I looked at the fact that I didn't have a choice at that moment about whether or not I was going to be robbed, I didn't have a choice about whether or not I was going to be raped. The only choice I had, really, was how unpleasant I was going to make this for myself. So I started with the point of view that I was a part of this, and that I had some power to influence the outcome.

"Although I didn't experience how I could be the source of this event, I was willing to take that point of view that I played some part in it. I was certainly willing to take the point of view that I could still cause something worthwhile to happen. Or at least cause something less destructive to happen.

"I didn't think of myself as a victim. I communicated with the people who were doing this thing. I recognized they were acting out of their own fear, that they desperately needed money, and that they were reacting to their feelings of being victims themselves. I looked at facilitating them, because I recognized their own terror and I knew that terrified people can do terrible things. I also knew I could choose to be more terrified than they were, in which case my friend and I might be killed. Or I could recognize their fear and recognize that the circumstances demanded that I learn some immediate lessons. Perhaps the lesson in front of me was to discover that I do have some power and that I do have some way of influencing events.

"They needed money, and wanted to take a lot of jewelry, which turns into money very inefficiently. They didn't get enough money from our two purses, so

I said I'd write them a check. They named a sum of money which was ridiculous, so I said to them, 'Look, it's no good writing a check for that amount because the check will bounce, and you'll be even more upset. I can write you a check for three hundred dollars and I promise I won't cancel it.' They were amazed, but they agreed and I got my jewelry back.

"Then they made it clear that they were going to rape me. I said to myself, 'Okay, I haven't had sex in three months and I have the power to make the event very unpleasant or make it whatever it is.' So that's how I related to it. They were amazed. It actually took the terror and anger out of them. My friend, on the other hand, resisted and struggled and had a much worse time of it."

Here is a woman who, in the context of public opinion and individual reason, had every right to consider herself a total victim, and yet this remarkable and beautiful person didn't choose to see herself this way. She looked radiant.

By way of contrast, there was another woman in the workshop who considered herself—with a shade of arrogance—to be very evolved. She had written a screenplay about altered states of consciousness which she wanted to sell to the film community. The film community wasn't interested. She couldn't get her screenplay accepted. She also wanted to be an actress but couldn't gain acceptance and success as an actress either. She saw herself as a total victim of people who refused to appreciate how brilliant she really was and how wonderful her screenplay really was, or what a wonderful contribution she and it would make to people and to life.

This person looked miserable and haggard, and talked of suicide. Here is a woman who held herself as a victim, and who as a result felt absolutely powerless, and miserable, giving her beautiful face a pallor of ugliness.

The situation in which this person had cast herself is part and parcel of the entertainment industry. And yet here she is in Hollywood claiming victimhood in a workshop largely populated by people from the same industry, people who know that one must either learn to accept such events or not be a part of the industry.

On the other hand, here in the same workshop is a person, a woman, who could legitimately consider herself a victim, and yet didn't, and who handled a situation which by most people's standards represented a very unpleasant and frightening experience in such a way that she became enriched. Through being robbed and raped she experienced her own power.

These two stories illustrate for us the power of a viewpoint of accountability.

Our heritage, our programming, our upbringing, conspire to push us into the category of the second woman, that of the victim. That's the way we have been conditioned to see life, and construct our impoverished model of the world.

Most of us would look at the first woman and say, "How can she look at it that way? It's not right." Given our model, her response is unreasonable. And yet, she is radiant, beautiful, and her life is rich.

By the way, this woman told us that the police and the medical examiner tried to get her to see herself as a victim; for their own needs, of course, not hers. Nobody around her would stop to see that she was being empowered and served by her viewpoint.

She told us what she liked about Actualizations was that she actually got support for being alive. And that people here could hear her experience and not ridicule her viewpoint; they could listen to her story and recognize that, yes, here was a viewpoint that actually worked. Instead of reacting with shock and trying to change her viewpoint, people in the Actualizations workshop were open to receive her story and her viewpoint as a contribution.

## Behavior: A Commitment to Excellence

So a viewpoint of accountability is the first half of the answer to the question of how do we get out of the hole and how do we get our power back. The other half of the answer is to be found in acquiring the ability to manifest behavior that is consistent with the viewpoint. Most of us don't do our homework and we don't commit ourselves to excellence. A commitment to excellence involves us in a lot of work, in going that extra step, in giving it all we've got, in doing it wisely and well rather than expediently. We live in a society that's been raised on expediency, and expediency robs us of the development of the skills required to reach mastery.

I've seen people who think they have acquired an evolved viewpoint but who have never manifested the skills of excellence in day-to-day living. This would be my criticism of the human potential movement in general. I've never seen an event in the human potential movement as well produced as "The Tonight Show" is five nights a week, on NBC, a show that these "evolved" people tend to look down on. We must recognize not only the value, but also the absolute necessity of acquiring the practical skills required to manage our relationship with reality.

We need to understand the nature of money, for example, how to manage it, the laws that govern it, and the skills required in working with it. It's the same with sex; we need to become aware of all the things we need to learn for sex to be a pleasure for us rather than an issue. If we look at our relationships, if we look at our communication, if we look at our work, the same holds true.

All aspects of our life, if our life is to be successful in any real way, require a level of skill and mastery. The word actualization means something made real through action. What we're going to do in the rest of this book is to look at viewpoints and skills that have to be acquired to really get our lives to work, in all areas.

# 5

# On Emotions and Feelings

In a little while we will talk about some specific things you can do that will allow you to free yourself from the tyranny of your fears. However, before we do that, let us take some time to talk generally about emotions and feelings.

Some of our emotions and feelings are genuinely appropriate responses to situations in our life. If somebody close to us dies, to be sad is a natural and appropriate response. In fact, not to be sad would be inappropriate. Sometimes someone very close to us will die and we will not be able to experience or express sadness. And we will feel guilty, because we do not experience sadness. The reason, of course, that we don't experience sadness is because we have, over the years, suppressed our ability to experience anything.

Not only have we suppressed our ability to experience emotions and feelings, we live in a culture which doesn't encourage us to do so. Rather the culture encourages us *not* to. As we mentioned earlier in the book, our culture doesn't give us very much permission, if any at all, to experience anything other than being "up." The culture doesn't give us permission to be down or sad. The culture doesn't give us permission to be depressed.

## Freedom Is Not Permission

Not that the culture's job, by the way, is to give us permission to do anything. I see it as an aberration that we have come to regard freedom as permission. Most people, when they say they want to be free, are actually seeking unlimited permission to do anything they feel like doing. "Please, Mommy, can I do this?" "Please, Daddy, can I do this?" "Please, Teacher, can I do this?" "Please, Mr. President, can we do this?" And so people's interpretation of freedom is reflected in their pursuit of permission.

Once we begin to seek freedom as permission, then whether we get permission or not has a major impact on our life. Let's take an emotion like sadness. Say something happens in our life and we get sad. The culture says, "Big boys don't cry." The culture says, "Now, now, dear, it'll be all right. You just have a cookie and a cup of tea, or lie down." Or it says, "C'mon, cheer up, it can't be that bad." The moment we begin to feel sad, somebody tries to take our sadness away from us. Somebody tries to make it better. It has been that way since our childhood. It is that way now. When we are not allowed to experience our sadness, we find ways to suppress it and not deal with it.

Anger is another good example. You can cite numerous phrases that go along with the suppression of our experience of anger: "Don't be angry," "It's not nice to display anger," "People won't like you," "Learn to control yourself," "What's wrong with you anyway?"

When our emotions and feelings are suppressed, something very damaging to our emotional health begins to happen. We won't be able to be angry when it's time to be angry, or sad when it's time to be sad.

Instead, suddenly we will find ourselves, for inexplicable reasons, bursting forth with a great deal of anger or sadness when it doesn't look like there is anything in our present environment that warrants the kind of intensity of emotion we are experiencing.

Imagine that our emotions and feelings are droplets of liquid collecting in a cup. If we experience our sadness when it's time to be sad, then the cup is being emptied. If we experience our anger when it's appropriate to experience anger, then the cup is being emptied. But when we don't experience sadness when it is time to experience sadness—when we keep our sadness suppressed—it stays in the cup. Each time we suppress our sadness, the cup fills up—drop by drop. Then one day the most insignificant little drop of sadness becomes enough to cause the emotion to flow over the sides like a waterfall. One seemingly insignificant incident can cause us to tap into a hidden reservoir of long-suppressed emotion.

The same is true with anger. If we've suppressed our experience of anger, we will have a cup full of anger. In this case, we will feel chronically resentful or hostile, because anger, when it is unexpressed, becomes resentment and covert hostility—an emotional tone injurious to our health.

One day a little additional drop of anger will go into the cup, and suddenly we will become enraged over a totally insignificant incidental event in our life. A torrent of anger will pour out, which is absolutely inappropriate to the circumstances, often with devastatingly damaging results. This, then, reinforces our opinion that we'd better suppress our anger even more.


## What It Means to Experience Your Emotions

We've all grown up with input telling us to suppress our emotions and feelings. As a result, we haven't allowed ourselves to experience our emotions and feelings. As a matter of fact, most of us don't even know what it means fully to experience our emotions and feelings.

First of all, full experience requires that we adopt a viewpoint of accountability. What does this mean? It means that we don't blame anybody else for our emotions and our feelings. (It is literally impossible, by the way, for one person to cause another to have an emotion or feeling.) As we discovered before, we've been conditioned to blame everybody else for our emotions and feelings. In fact, we've been conditioned to blame everybody else for everything.

This is an insidious habit. The habit begins with our parents—unknowingly—teaching us that somebody else causes our emotions and feelings. Mommy says, "Why do you upset Mommy so?" Father says, "Your grades are a disappointment to the whole family. You make me ashamed of you." Even the statement, "You make me so happy—you did so well," implies "blame."

Learning is a process of interaction with the external environment. We learn everything as a result of the feedback we get. We modify our behavior in an attempt to secure the desired feedback.

All the feedback we get as children tells us that our emotions and feelings are caused by something or somebody outside of us, and that we are not responsible for our responses. There's no experience of ownership. In the face of what we can't own, we are without power; we are without mastery.

If we stop and reflect for a while, it becomes apparent that we do own our emotions and feelings. After all, we don't experience anybody's else's emotions, and we don't experience anybody else's feelings.

We need to recognize that we really are accountable. That means to recognize that we are a part, cause, agent, or source of our emotions and our feelings. On that basis, once we recognize that they're ours—once we recognize that we're accountable for them, that they are part of *our* life—then we've owned another part of our life. We've also begun to regain our power.

Emotions and feelings are a part of life. If you're alive, you have them. Not to own them is to give up your personal power to them. To experience your emotions and feelings means, for example, to allow yourself to feel sad when you're sad, rather than to automatically try to do something about it.

This means going against the cultural current which is telling us so strongly that we'd better do something to feel better. Next time, don't do anything to feel better. Just be sad when it's time to be sad. This doesn't mean that you should go around complaining, or inflicting your sadness on everybody else. It is certainly all right to communicate to others that you are sad; just be clear that you do not expect or want them to try "and make it better." Now may be a time to be quiet and be by yourself. It may be a time to go for long walks or to sit in a garden or wade along the seashore.

A key to accepting the richness of your own emotional life lies in knowing that it's really all right to be sad. Sadness is a part of life. Our emotions and feelings make us human beings. There are always going to be events in our life that will be the catalyst for our experience of some part of the entire spectrum of emotions and feelings that we're able to experience.

If we deny our "negative" feelings, then at the same time unwittingly we effectively deny our ability to experience what we call "positive" feelings. It's an error, by the way, to call sadness a negative feeling. Sadness is absolutely not a negative feeling. In fact, when you can allow yourself to fully experience your sadness, you can find a kind of quiet beauty in it. If you can allow yourself to experience sadness appropriately, you'll find that it's an experience you want to have. You will find that, in fact, you don't want somebody to make it better.

When you fully embrace your own sadness, you will

experience, on the other side of your sadness, a deep and rich sense of compassion for all humanity.

## For Prompt Temporary Relief, in Many Cases

If we suppress our emotions and feelings long enough it becomes habitual. If we continue, it becomes chronic. For example, if our sadness is suppressed and not experienced, our cup begins to fill up and, if we continue long enough, sadness will dominate our whole life. Our life will be seen through a veil of sadness. Ironically, the very emotion that we seek to deny becomes the lens through which we view the world, for the very denial reinforces the feeling and it becomes ever-present.

Owning our emotions and feelings enables us to begin to gain some mastery over them—and regain some of our own power. For instance, if we are afraid, we don't have to react automatically to our fear as if the fear is justified. We can be afraid, without reacting to avoid the fear, without becoming a Don Quixote fighting windmills.

We can be sad without acting sad. We can be angry without acting angrily. We can be insecure without acting insecure. We can be frightened without acting frightened.

Not only can we—we *must*, if we are to be mentally, emotionally, and physically healthy.

This returns us to the very important principle we explored earlier. We'll restate it: *Every time we act, we reinforce the motivating emotion, feeling, attitude, or belief behind the action.* The long-term consequence of our behavior always reinforces the emotion, feeling, attitude, or belief that motivated the behavior in the first place.

Acting out an emotion or feeling is like using Preparation H for hemorrhoids. We may get prompt, temporary relief in many cases, but the hemorrhoids don't go away, although our experience of them may be suppressed for a while.

Most of the prescriptions we try for relief from our emotions and feelings are really our particular version of Preparation H. Although we avoid the unwanted experience temporarily, we develop into long-term chronic sufferers. In accordance with the principle that all action reinforces the motivating emotion or feeling behind the action, matters get worse. It is like taking aspirin for a headache that is actually caused by a brain tumor. For a while the aspirin will work on the pain, but you still die of a brain tumor.

What we ordinarily do with our emotions and feelings is pursue the expedient albeit temporary benefit. We seek to avoid the pain and to pursue the temporary benefit of being comfortably the effect of our own avoidance behavior. For example: If we feel anger, and then, as a result, act angrily, we become the short-term effect of our own behavior, providing ourselves with a sense of relief. "Boy, I feel better now. I let off steam," we say to ourselves. (There are systems of therapy based on such discharges.) However, in the long run, we become the effect of our behavior in a destructive way.

By acting out of anger we *avoid* the experience of being angry, but others become angry, and we add to the total volume of anger we carry around in our "cup." We feel "better" because our behavior relieves the pressure of our feelings and we avoid some of the intensity of our discomfort. But our angry behavior doesn't do anything to *resolve the source* of the anger.

## Why We Get Angry

Let's look at the mechanics of why we get angry. Let's say that we are being angry because somebody doesn't treat us well. Why does that "make" us angry?

Because we think they should have more respect for us?

Okay, but why does *that* "make" us angry?

We always get back to the same answer: FEAR. Our anger is our "fight" reaction to our fear. Our fear is that we *are* unworthy, and we interpret the bad treatment we receive as a valid indictment of our unworthiness. Our fear is that we are treated badly because we really *are* bad, or that we are treated with disrespect because we are not worthy of respect.

Acting angrily when we feel angry will serve to alienate the other person. Our angry behavior will, in effect, provide the other person with a justification for treating us badly in the first place. After all, we are now proving to him that he was justified in treating us badly by behaving in a way that is unworthy of consideration and respect.

## Resolving the Source of Our Anger

Let's say that it's true that somebody treated us badly, that they were just plain rude and inconsiderate. We feel angry. Our anger is a function of our thinking that they have just made a valid statement about us. We are angry because we are afraid. Remember, the two automatic solutions to fear are fight or flight. Our anger is a fight reaction to fear. Unfortunately, these short-term solutions of flight or fight create a long-term reality that our fears are valid.

The dynamic goes something like this: We get treated badly. Then we create our experience of anger because we are afraid—we're afraid that we really are so worthless that we warrant being treated badly. Also, because we've been conditioned to react with anger, we are further prompted to feel angry if somebody treats us badly. If we do what we ordinarily do— blindly act out anger—we may get prompt temporary relief, but we will, in the long run, reinforce our propensity for anger *and* our feelings of unworthiness.

The fear that we are unworthy is the motivating principle behind our angry behavior. We behave angrily in an attempt to avoid the experience of our fear that we are in fact unworthy.

## How to Restore Your Power

Now let's see how we can look at the whole situation differently, and how this shift in our point of view can restore our power.

Imagine that you have just been treated badly and that you are now angry. Let's say that this time, instead of acting out your anger, you say to yourself:

"Wait a minute. I just got treated badly, and now I'm beginning to get angry. Well, perhaps the way this person is relating to me doesn't have anything to do with me at all. Perhaps the fact that this person is treating me badly is not a statement about me; it's a statement about him. What he is actually telling me about himself is that he is a person who, when he feels badly, treats others badly. Because this person feels bad, he is now acting badly towards me."

(Of course, the possibility also exists that you have unwittingly treated him badly, in which case be gracious and apologize.)

Now we've turned the whole situation around. We're willing to see this other person's behavior in terms of the statement his behavior makes about him, rather than just seeing the situation from our own narrow, fearful, self-interested point of view. And now we will feel totally different. We will feel empowered, rather than victimized.

When we act angrily, we give up our power to whatever object we are using as an excuse for acting angrily. Because once our internal reaction of anger is externalized and we are out of control, we've lost power. When we are out of control, we don't have any power in our life.

Indeed, our angry behavior reflects our fear of powerlessness. Our out-of-control, angry behavior will, in the long run, reinforce our feelings of powerlessness, because by being the effect of our internal reactions of anger we give up our power to our feelings, thereby making them stronger and us weaker.

In the angry moment, we are powerless—reinforcing and making real our fear of being powerless—which is why we got angry in the first place!

Anger is an instinctive reaction. The fight reaction to fear is part of our genetic makeup. But the key to retrieving our own power lies in our ability to become bigger than this instinct.

Now, it's true that, as Will Durant said, our instincts were formed during a thousand centuries of insecurity, but be that as it may, we do have the real option to rise above our oppressive inheritance. If we are willing to look at another person's behavior towards us as a reflection of the state of their relationship with themselves rather than as a statement about our value as a person, then we will, over a period of time, cease to react at all.

Once again, we are going to restate our principle, a little differently this time. *We always react internally before we react externally. In other words, we're going to experience internal reaction first. If we make the internal reaction external, then the external reaction will reinforce the internal reaction, making this kind of reaction more common in the future.*

All emotions and feelings are either internal *responses* or internal *reactions*. An internal response is almost always appropriate and ought to be experienced, explored, and expressed. An internal reaction is usually inappropriate and ought to be examined. It should not be allowed to become the motivating principle behind our behavior.

Inevitably, internal reactions become external reactions. And, internal reactions that are externalized will be reinforced by the externalization of the reaction.

An internal reaction of anger, if externalized, will reinforce the frequency and intensity of angry internal reactions.

For most people, the externalization of their internal reactions is unfortunately automatic. But we do have another option, and that is to observe our internal reaction instead of automatically going from internal reaction to external manifestation of the internal reaction.

There is always a moment in time between the internal reaction and the externalization of the internal reaction. And it's in that moment that we have choice. The power to change our life exists in that moment between internal reaction and the externalization of the internal reaction. That's the *moment of power*. When you claim this moment of power, you are free to act, rather than react. Remember, power is the ability to act.

Please be clear that we are not suggesting that you suppress your anger or any of your other emotions and feelings. To do so is definitely injurious to your mental, emotional, and physiological health. What we are talking about here, and in the pages that follow, is experiencing your responses, emotions, and feelings in a responsible way. The goal is for you to have your emotions and feelings and at the same time relate productively to other people.

The result will be a richer experience of the emotions and feelings you want (i.e., love, happiness, and strength) and the abatement of the painful emotions and feelings you don't want.

# 6

# On How to Make Painful Emotions and Feelings Productive

### What Is Jealousy?

We will now explore a productive way of relating to the phenomenon we call jealousy.

When we are jealous, we usually become reactive and absolutely powerless. We are completely neutralized, unable to cause what we want to happen to happen. Jealousy is a fear reaction, it is a reaction to our feelings of the fear of impending loss, usually the loss of love and support, and perhaps to the underlying fear that we are unlovable. We may also have a chronic fear that anyone we love and make important will always leave us. When we react out of our feelings of jealousy, we actually cause to happen that which we desire most not to happen. *This demonstrates the dynamic of our principle in action; that the idea or feeling behind our behavior will be reinforced by the behavior itself.*

### Scenario #1: The Flight Reaction

Let's start with a scenario. As we go through this little example, picture yourself in the appropriate role.

You are involved in what the world calls a monogamous, committed relationship with someone with whom you are "in love." The two of you are at a party. You separate yourself from your lover to fetch some drinks. When you return you find your partner deeply involved in what appears to be an intimate conversation with a charming member of the opposite sex. It is with someone who appears to have all the qualities which you are afraid you do not have enough of.

They seem to be having a wonderful time together. You, on the other hand, feel a sudden contraction in your stomach, your mind races, you feel angry, threatened. You know deep down that you should not feel this way so you suppress your feelings. You become quiet and withdrawn. The real you, along with all the attractive qualities of the real you, disappears. You have modified your behavior in reaction to your feelings of jealousy.

Your reaction is the suppression of your normal sense of humor; it is the suppression of your normal playfulness and affability. All the qualities that your lover likes about you have either vanished or are about to vanish. Now, what do you suppose will happen if you continue to suppress all the qualities that your partner likes about you? Your relationship will deteriorate. And how will you act when the relationship begins to deteriorate? You will probably become either more withdrawn, or hostile, and further suppress all the qualities that your partner likes about you.

Now if that charming other person is still around, who will clearly look the more attractive of the two of you? Exactly. So what is likely to happen is that your greatest fears will come true. Your lover will leave you for another person, which will reinforce your original belief that you are not good enough, that you're not worthy of another's affections, and that you don't deserve a good relationship. You will begin to believe that you conned your partner into loving you in the first place, and that he or she is about to find out that he or she has been conned.

All of this represents your *flight* reaction to your fear. In this case, you exhibit withdrawal and self-suppression with perhaps some hostility.

## Scenario #2: The Fight Reaction

Now, let's take another scenario. This one includes the *fight* reaction to jealousy rather than the flight, withdrawal reaction to jealousy.

Let's say that you and your partner both work in different fields. You both agreed earlier in the day that you were going to eat dinner together at home. You arrive home a little early, so you decide to make dinner. Your partner has promised to be home at seven-thirty, so you time dinner for eight. (I will now use the female pronoun for this story, but please feel free to change the gender to suit your preference.) Here's what happens: She doesn't get home until eleven. Her hair is mussed and her clothes look as though she slept in them. And she didn't call. What do you think will happen next? You will probably demand to know where she has been and why she didn't call.

Let's say that she tells you that it's her life and she doesn't have to answer to you for her whereabouts. As a consequence of your next reaction she may find that she is now wearing dinner instead of eating it. You may now turn every available unattached object in the kitchen into an airborne armada in her direction.

Now, why are you upset; what is it that you are afraid of? What you are afraid of is the truth about her behavior this evening: That she made love with somebody else? And, if she did, what meaning does this hold for you? That you're not enough, perhaps?

Okay, now, let's look at all the possibilities here. One possibility, of course, is that she didn't make love to anybody else. There is a perfectly innocent explanation to her lateness and disheveled appearance. But let's forget about that one because it only happens on

"I Love Lucy," and for most of us this is just too good to be true.

Let's say that exactly what you are afraid of has happened. She met a man who was tremendously attractive to her, and he asked her out for a quick drink. He just happened to have a wonderful condominium overlooking the water, and just around the corner; he invited her to admire his etchings and they made love.

Now, let's ask, why did she do this? What is the motivating idea or feeling behind her behavior? Well, it could be that she had some doubts about her own sexuality. She may have felt insecure sexually and didn't really know if she was a good lover. Along came this handsome man who looked tremendously accomplished, so she thought that if she could make love to him in a way that would please and satisfy him that would mean she was a great lover. So she did what she did out of her own fears concerning her own sexuality.

In other words, her behavior does not represent some kind of statement about you. It does not reflect her judgment of you. It simply represents the externalization of her fears about herself in the area of her own sexuality. Thus her behavior isn't personal with respect to you.

Of course, it's almost impossible to look at it this way under these circumstances. It's a pity that it is so difficult, because if we can look at it this way, we would see that it is an opportunity to really make a difference.

Let's take this a few steps further. Let's say that sexually she did have a very good experience with this person. And she did in fact resolve with him some of her misgivings about her own sexuality. If that did happen, you are very likely to be one of the beneficiaries. This is a difficult concept for most of us to realize, but any insecurity that she has about herself sexually will detract from the quality of the sexual relationship you have together. To the extent that she

has insecurities about her own sexuality, she won't be
able to be present for you sexually. Her fears will be
there instead. If her fears are dissolved, and she
becomes sexually more alive, you will be a benefi-
ciary.

To continue, let's say that she had a fine and satisfying sexual experience with this man, and that she now
comes in the front door and is very confused. She feels
on some level that what she did is a violation of her
commitment to you.

It needn't be, by the way. I have perhaps a very
strange point of view to put forward here. I'm not
advocating promiscuity, but let's say that this in fact is
the scenario. She was insecure about her own sexuality; she consciously recognized that, and also recognized that it must cost you something in your relationship together. She saw an opportunity to perhaps get
beyond some of her own sexual misgivings with this
man. She took the opportunity and indeed she did get
beyond many of her misgivings. So she came home to
you more able to be with you sexually. Now ask
yourself: Has she violated her committment to the
relationship? My answer is no, not necessarily, indeed
if she is now more fully able to love you sexually, she
has honored it.

This represents a radical point of view, because our
current society says her behavior is bad. As we shall
see later on, other cultures have had very different
ways of looking at such events. We have to decide
whether we are going to make a commitment to the
quality of our experience in life or a commitment to the
way the culture believes things are supposed to look.
Most people end up making their commitment to the
way they believe things should look. Very few people
survive their childhood with their commitment to life
intact. Because a commitment to life is a commitment
to experiencing life—all of it. This is a commitment
that requires us to go beyond our existing limits to
resolve our fears about ourselves and life.

Meanwhile, back at the kitchen, your partner has come in the front door. On some level she knows that the events of the evening have been good for her. But by the same token she cannot have lived in our culture and remained isolated and immune from its conditioning and so-called moral standards. So, a part of her, even though she may intellectually know better, may be feeling guilty. She will perhaps feel that she has violated the relationship. She will have mixed feelings, because on the one hand she had a good time, but on the other hand she knows that she loves you. Given existing cultural realities, she is bound to be experiencing conflict.

Now, if you at this point, turn on her in anger you will only succeed in providing her with an absolute justification for her behavior. By your aggressive reaction she can now make you wrong enough to make her behavior in the last few hours right, and justifying that she was where she was. And you have provided her with an incentive to return to the situation with the other man. And what was your fear in the first place? It was that you weren't good enough. And if in fact she leaves you, what will you have established? Right. That you're not good enough.

So once again we see a classic case of the behavior reinforcing the fear underlying the behavior, setting in action a whole series of events that reinforce the feeling that you are not good enough.

Now, let's take the scenario a step further. She does in fact leave; she goes off with the other man. How will you feel now? That you are not good enough. And when you go on to the next relationship, will you go into it from a position of greater relative strength than the last relationship, or greater relative weakness? Weakness. What then is likely to happen in the next relationship? The scenario will be repeated and your fear will become further reinforced.

This is how we keep creating our own personal reality. We create and re-create the personal reality of our lives in reaction to which we develop our "personality" that further reinforces the personal reality of our lives which then further reinforces our "personality."

At this point you may say to yourself, "This is all very easy for you to write about, but can anybody actually live in the real world responsively rather than reactively, on a regular basis?"

The answer is yes, they can, and yes, you can. The principles we are exploring are relatively simple, although living them does take discipline and work.

In order to respond rather than react to the first scenario, allow yourself to become aware of your growing internal reaction. Next, recognize and exercise choice in the moment of power between your internal reaction and the externalization of your internal reaction.

Instead of suppressing yourself, thereby making yourself less appealing as a person, do whatever you can do to be the way you really are. Now you might be a little subdued for a while, but the chances are that once you see the situation for what it is, you will recognize the foolishness and the unworkability of your own reaction and self-suppression in the situation. Then it will be possible for you to be more yourself. It is critical here that whenever you catch yourself about to behave reactively that you do not do so. To the extent you are more yourself, you've lowered the risk of damaging your relationship in the current situation.

We will now return to the second scenario, a situation in which our jealousy may be considered justified. As far as I'm concerned, by the way, there's no such thing as justified jealousy. Of course, in the eyes of the world there is justified jealousy. However, the concept "justified" is a trap.

We talked before about the way a woman in the Actualizations Workshop responded to being robbed and raped. She responded, rather than reacted, in a way that wasn't "justified." In the world's reality it would have been justified for her to have been outraged, angry, and upset, and had she done that during the event she probably would have gotten killed. In life, if you insist on conducting yourself in a way that may popularly be considered justified and right, you may just find that you end up literally dead right!

This second scenario is one in which you could easily fall into the trap of justified jealousy and a set of series of deadening reactions. Here we are looking for practical ways to utilize the moment of power to respond and build our relationship rather than to react and destroy it.

Let's begin with the awful possibility that your worst fears have come true. Not only was she with somebody else, but it also turns out that he is a wonderful lover and an absolute joy to be with. He falls in love with her and she falls in love with him, and they decide to run off together in the hope of living happily ever after.

If that's what happened, you are going to be hurt and upset. If your relationship together has been important to you, then you are going to have to spend some time experiencing being hurt and upset. Life does contain these events without your necessarily contributing to them through your behavior.

But let's say that she comes in the door. Rather than reacting, you could say, "I'm glad you are home. And I'm really upset that you are late. It looks to me like you are upset too. Is there something that you want to talk about?" You have to become bigger than your own emotions and feelings in this moment to make this a moment of power. You've acknowledged that you have strong emotions and feelings, but you are not going to use them as the motivation behind reactive behavior.

Before proceeding further, we had better examine another important set of relationships between fear, lies, and the truth. What many people would do when questioned under the circumstances we've described is lie. In fact, under these circumstances, if you were in your partner's shoes, you would feel at least some pressure to lie. But, why do we lie to each other? (Remember, anything less than the truth is a lie.)

We lie because of our fear. We lie as a solution to our fear of the way that somebody else will react to a truth we may tell them that they don't like. We lie because we are afraid of having to cope with somebody else's very negative or even violent reaction to us, after we present to them a truth that they find very upsetting.

The other side of this is that if we want to be a partner who isn't lied to in a relationship, then we had better be a person who responds, but does not react, to unwelcome news. If you have consistently related to your partner in such a way that she knows that it is safe to tell you the truth, and if you consistently respond to your partner's input from the point of view of seeking what serves both of you as growing people, then a reality becomes established in your partner's experience that it is productive, rather than danger- ous, to tell you the truth. We all need to remember that in any form of relationship, we will not be lied to if it is established in the other person's mind that we can be trusted not to use his truths in evidence against him.

Notice, in fact, that we do have all sorts of fears about another person's reaction to our truths that they may not like or may find upsetting. It may be our fear of being judged, our fear of their being violent towards us, our fear of their saying, "I'm not going to play with you anymore," or, "You are a terrible person." We may fear withdrawal of material support; withdrawal of privileges, withdrawal of affection, of closeness, of what we call love. All of these fears may be based on past real experiences.

## How to Respond Instead of React

But let's imagine that in this current situation you say, "I'm glad to see you are home. I'm upset, and I indulged in my own fears about your uncommunicated absence. Anyhow, what's really happening?" She may say, "Well, I don't want to talk about it right now." To which you could say, "Well, I can see that you are upset. That's fine. Do you want to eat? Or should I have a banquet by myself?"

This gives her the most room to become responsive rather than reactive. Because anything that you do that will result in the intensification of her fear will only compound your problems, and her problems, and will precipitate a deterioration, at least temporarily and perhaps permanently, in the relationship.

Another possibility is that she might say, "Okay, I have a terrible thing to tell you," and then blurts out what happened. (That's assuming that she is in a place where she thinks that what she did was terrible.)

The way for you to look at this, assuming that you do value the relationship, is from the viewpoint of what will serve the relationship with her. This will require that you contribute to the way that she feels about herself. Because if she shares with you that she did what she did, then you have to explore the motivating feelings, attitudes, and ideas behind her behavior this evening.

Awful Possibility Number One is that she really doesn't think that you are a very good lover. Or she found that the sexual relationship with you wasn't all that she hoped for, and she didn't know whether it was you or her. Moreover, she felt unable to talk to you about this. So part of her motivation for going elsewhere was to find out whether or not she had sexual blocks limiting her sexual fulfillment.

She may have found out that indeed most of her sexual disappointment was a consequence of her own insecurities or imagined inadequacies. Or she may have discovered that she is a wonderful, responsive lover, and therefore now feels that you are suppressed sexually. In which case, as uncomfortable as you may feel, you need to take corrective action.

If this is the case, the events of the evening are a signal for creative action on your part rather than a destructive and angry reaction we so often see in relationships in these circumstances.

We are of course assuming that you've got what people refer to as a committed monogamous relationship, which is the prevailing cultural model. (This is not to say that committed monogamy is necessarily an appropriate or desirable model for you, but we will leave this aside for a while.) If you are conducting a social experiment called "Does sexual monogamy work?" your partner's evening activity is a violation of this. Here then is a signal that creative introspection and action are required.

You must see this sequence of events, as painful as it might be, as a challenge and an opportunity, rather than as an irrefutable indictment of your inadequacies as a lover and as a person. You've got to see it as a challenge that requires either or both of you to be bigger than your fear, and more skilled, more open, more spontaneous, and more creative in some area, the specific area in this case being human sexuality.

Another possibility is that your partner may have felt that there was something missing in your sexual relationship, and she decided to go exploring. She now arrives home devastated, because though her new lover was sexually very experienced in his sexual skills, he was also very arrogant and very "macho," with the result that your partner became sexually and emotionally intimidated and didn't perform well at all.

(Not that I think that sex is simply a performance. Indeed, I think that it is ridiculous to consider sex as a performance. People talk about sexual adequacy, but adequacy is fundamentally an engineering term. It seems to be very inappropriate to use an engineering term as an adjective in the area of human sexuality.)

Your partner may have come away from the evening's encounter absolutely convinced that sexually she's terribly inadequate. She may wonder how, with all her "problems," you could possibly want to have a relationship with her.

So while it is true that you feel hurt and perhaps angry, at the same time it is true that you have in front of you a person who is also hurting, a person who feels even more inadequate than you had begun to feel in the presence of your own fear. So now the opportunity for you is to grow bigger than your feelings, to move beyond your own personal difficulty in the situation and look at how you can be your partner's friend. Because, at this moment, she doesn't need the soap-opera-style portrayal of the "wronged lover." She needs a friend. We need not only to be our partner's lover, we need also to be our partner's friend.

It appears to me that if a relationship between a man and a woman is to endure, it must be built on a friendship laced with a sense of humor and good sex. And—as is currently the case—the area of good sex is often an area of difficulty. What is needed here is the warmth and healing power of friendship, compassion, and a sense of humor.

We must also discover what action needs to be taken. Because it may be that your partner is sexually alive, or it may be that she isn't, and if she isn't, then corrective action can be taken. It may call for both of you to seek the support of a very competent facilitator in this area. There are psychologists and psychiatrists who specialize in the field of human sexuality. Or you just may need to take time to behold each other's bodies differently as you creatively approach each other's sexual fears and fantasies.

Let's return to the possibility that she may have found out that she's fine and that you are not doing too well. You will probably now feel that you are under a tremendous amount of pressure, in fact more pressure than most of us can respond to, the kind of pressure that we almost always react to. But beyond the reaction that you may feel is the lesson you must learn. You have to pay attention to your own growth sexually. This may require that you enlist the support of a competent therapist and do the necessary growth work for yourself, so that sex becomes a pleasure instead of an issue.

It's important to recognize once again that if you play out the typical B-grade-movie scenario of angrily hurling everything available in the kitchen at her, it is unlikely that you will have contributed to the relationship. It will in fact give your partner something to use as a justification for her behavior. And that will provide her with an incentive to be with somebody else. The very behavior you are upset about will have been reinforced by your angry reaction. In this way you will make your fears come true.

That's the lesson here. And it is a lesson that we must learn, as difficult and painful as it may be.

Frequently in relationships we struggle to hold each other in line; we manipulate and suppress our partner by holding the relationship hostage. It is a subtle form of blackmail. We do it in essence by saying, "If you violate our relationship, if you sleep with somebody other than me, I will be so upset that I will leave," which is another way of saying, "I will kill the relationship." It is a form of commitment by threat. And it takes all the choice, and therefore all the life, out of our relationships.

We must recognize that the need we feel to blackmail each other in such fashion comes out of our fear. Because underneath the struggle for dominance and control lies our fear that we are not enough; the fear that just the way we are is not enough for our partner to want to be with us. We forget (if indeed we ever consciously knew in the first place) that most relationships are about the coming together of two frightened people. In these circumstances the only time the relationship is real is when it is functioning beyond our reactions to fear.

Most relationships are about two people who are not making it alone, trying to make it together. The two partners add each other's fear to their own fear. In this way they get a double helping of fear. They get their own fear plus their partner's fear, either directly or by osmosis. Such a situation is bound to become destructive.

The key to your power to transform your own situation is to address yourself compassionately to your partner's fear instead of indulging in and reacting to your own. If you keep focused on supporting your partner's sense of self, as opposed to your seeking dominance, then out of that focus will come a dialogue that will be creative. If you get lost in the indulgence of and the reaction to your own fears, you will be inflicting your fear on top of your partner's fear, and things will get worse.

What we are talking about is a tremendous challenge to grow and to be a big person. A lot of people don't rise to the challenge. Resolve that you will number among the few who do. You can if you want to. Use your moment of power between internal reaction and external reactive behavior.

### Enriching Your Ability to Build Extraordinary Relationships

Once again we must pause to remember that we can't live beyond our means. Each scenario we have explored offers an opportunity for us to enrich our means to build an extraordinary relationship.

If you transcend, rise above, or become bigger than your own fear and your reaction to that fear, then you will find your experience of yourself expanded beyond your ability to imagine. You will experience that you are empowered. You will have enriched your means to have a phenomenal relationship. I guarantee it; I've seen this happen.

You can respond rather than react. You can nourish rather than censure. You can support rather than condemn.

## If You Don't Hate Me, You Don't Love Me

Sometimes we have partners whose reality is such that they believe that they should be judged and punished by being treated harshly. They may interpret your failure to react in outrage and treat them harshly as meaning that you don't love them. They may believe that if you really loved them, you would be insanely jealous and very angry. They may expect to be beaten or at least have the kitchen thrown at them. (Such a view reflects the popular mythology.) Because you don't do that they may think that you don't love them, and they will leave.

I've had that happen to me. It looked as though I lost what I wanted because I would not behave in a way that reinforced the popular but destructive mythology, and my friend was used to always being reacted to. But, on the other side of the loss, I recognized that I had no business being in a relationship with a person who was not ready to receive being treated well.

## Going for What Works

As difficult as it may seem at first, we have got to go for what will work in the long run, rather than what we want for immediate gratification. One day we must realize that we want what works.

Most people go for what they think they want. Such wants are almost always reactive and never ultimately satisfying. When we stop going for what we think we want and go instead for what will work, we may feel deprived for a while, but on the other side of the temporary deprivation is long-term satisfaction, the recognition we got what we really did want, and our own power.

We will keep coming back to our principle: *Every time we act we reinforce the motivating feeling, atti-*

*tude, or belief behind the act.* While the short-term consequences of reacting may feel good in the moment, it is the long-term consequences of not reacting that are beneficial, for they will change our life. Note that the short-term consequences of not reacting may be uncomfortable, especially at first as we begin to alter the way we function in life.

However, this discomfort can be used to our benefit. By becoming aware of and examining the exact nature of the feelings that make up our discomfort we are able to become aware of the motivating attitudes, ideas, and feelings behind what would have become our behavior. In this way, as we isolate our negative and impoverishing attitudes and ideas, we can begin to free ourselves by examining them rather than acting on them.

## How to Win Friends and Influence Destiny

Dale Carnegie wrote about people's need to feel important. Much of Carnegie's system with which to "win friends and influence people" is based upon techniques to make people feel important. And it works. The only thing wrong with the system is that it works only superficially. It works to perpetuate our own and other people's insecurities. It works to allow us to rise to the top of the pile that is built on superficiality, as much of our culture is.

But the system doesn't produce a long-term experience of real human closeness and true friendship. If we win "friends" and influence people through catering to their need to be important, they may "love" us and we will perhaps become successful, but only so long as we cater to their need to feel important—i.e., to their insecurities.

We are not supporting these people in any real way, because their need to feel important comes out of their feeling that they are not worthy of respect. Every time we cater to their need to feel important by trying to make them feel important, we are, in fact, reinforcing their fear that they are unimportant. So their low self-esteem is further perpetuated. While we may attain some level of success, we will also feel insecure, because we will be carrying the fear that if we stop being a source of their feeling important, then they will suddenly stop being our "friends." We simply cannot build anyone's sense of self-worth in this way, including our own.

It may be that we are collecting friends because we think they are the kinds of friends that will make us important in the world—we can also find ourselves doing the same thing with job titles. Here is a way of discovering if you are collecting relationships and job titles out of your need to feel important: Begin by noticing whether or not you are promoting or boasting about the fact that you have a relationship with an "important person" or that you have an impressive-sounding job title. If you are promoting or boasting about them, this is a telltale sign that deep down inside of you there is a person who feels unimportant.

This kind of behavior of course further reinforces your dependency on such props and further reinforces your very deep feelings that you are unimportant and not worthwhile. The most revealing test for what's really going on is to cease doing the things that we feel compelled to do. This takes awareness of our own behavior, and demands awareness of our own internal reactions that are the motivating force behind our behavior.

## Where to Find Your Power

If our own internal reactions are not witnessed by us and they go directly to an externalization of the reaction, then we don't have any power to change.

Your power begins with the awareness of what's happening. It exists in the moment between your internal reaction and the externalization of that reaction, the moment between experience and behavior.

Awareness alone doesn't produce change, but it gives you a choice, it offers you power. Whether or not you take advantage of the offer is up to you. Awareness is simply the opportunity for power; it can be the beginning of change.

Suppose that we become aware of our actions and notice that we have been promoting a relationship we have, or boasting about the fact that we've just been made a director of a successful business. Now, our promotional efforts may be appropriate to our true best interests—sometimes advertising works. On the other hand, the fact that we are out promoting could come out of a neurotic need we have to cater to our feelings that we are unimportant and unworthy of respect. If we are actually promoting because it's in our true best interest to promote, then when we stop promoting we will feel fine. If, however, we have been promoting the relationship or the job because deep down we feel unimportant, then when we stop promoting we will start to feel terrible. We will start to feel worthless, and that nobody's noticing us. We will start to feel that nobody thinks that we are important. We will start to feel that nobody's drawn or attracted to us.

## Enriching Your Life

Just as it's true that every time we act we reinforce the motivating feeling, attitude, or belief behind the act, the reverse is also true. Every time we *don't* act we diminish, and begin to free ourselves from, the motivating belief or feeling or attitude behind the action we were about to take.

If we refrain from externalizing our reactions we will, in the short term, experience an intensification of that motivating feeling, attitude, or belief. This can be very uncomfortable. But if we want to live a life of *internal* as well as external richness, we must be willing to endure the short-term discomforts. While we seem usually willing to go through the initial physical discomforts of training our bodies to perform new sporting activities, this willingness is often lacking when it comes to training our psyche. However, the rewards of our willingness to undertake this kind of inner fitness program are likely to surpass our most extravagant dreams!

## How Fear Begets Fear

Let's talk more about fear. We'll start by restating our principle in another way. *Any act of avoidance of a fear will reinfoce the fear.* Any act of avoidance reinforces the fear motivating the behavior.

There is a very old example of this principle. The English landed gentry, who spent much of their time hunting and jumping horses, always told their youngsters after they fell off a horse to get right back on. They knew (even if they didn't know why they knew) that if the child didn't get back on the horse and keep riding, he would grow up with an unwarranted and inappropriate fear of horses.

It is true, of course, that some fear is healthy because it gets us to show respect where respect should be appropriately shown. As we have said before, fear can steer us away from the things that are fundamentally injurious to our well-being. Horses are not fundamentally a threat, although some respect is prudent. I'm sure most of us are aware that if a child falls off a horse and does not get back on immediately, then the chances of his or her ever getting back on diminish with the passage of time. A number of the great automobile racing drivers have written that they have had to get back behind the wheel of a car and drive very hard as soon as possible after a bad accident if they were ever going to race successfully again. They knew that every day they put off getting back in the car and pushing themselves lessened the chances of their ever again being a world-class driver.

We have given our power over to our fear. If we are to become empowerd we must become conscious of those aspects of our behavior that present the avoidance of our fear. And we must cease our avoidance behavior; for to continue is to reinforce our fear, further eroding our power to live successfully.

Fear can spin a subtle web of our containment. By way of illustration, let us examine the story of Marcie.

Marice came to the Actualizations Workshop a woman afraid she was not good enough to be loved by a man. A woman who, while growing up, found that the only way she could win the affection of her father was by doing the things he thought women were supposed to do. But we are ahead of ourselves. Let's start at the beginning.

Marcie is the first-born child. Her father, who had really wanted a son, is immediately disappointed that she is not a boy. But in spite of his disappointment he soon learns to love her and begins to give her a lot of attention, because at this point he finds her beauty, curiosity, and playfulness irresistible. A truly alive baby can seduce almost all but the deadest of people into some experience of love and life. So she gets a lot of loving attention and is very happy.

But, deep down inside, Daddy still considers it a terrible mistake that she wasn't a boy. So Mommy and Daddy try again and, lo and behold, when Marcie is about three years of age, which is a very delicate time in her life, a boy arrives.

Well, Daddy's absolutely overjoyed and all the attention that was previously Marcie's now goes to the new male arrival. Her father's attention and love are there for the boy and abruptly no longer available to her. Marcie is terribly upset. She desperately begins to search for ways to regain Daddy's attention. Well, nothing seems to work.

Time passes, and Marcie and her brother are both

going to school. One day Marcie hears Daddy say that good grades are important, so she goes off and begins to get good grades. In fact, Marcie gets better grades than her brother. Father is not pleased. She can't understand why her outstanding grades do not receive his blessing. In fact, they instead seem to elicit Daddy's anger. Marcie has no way of knowing why Daddy is angry. She cannot know that in her father's reality boys are supposed to get the best grades. She cannot possibly know that in his mind her success makes her brother a failure, which angers him. In his belief system, girls are supposed to bake cakes, do the washing, make the beds, and not have sex before they are married.

So Marcie keeps trying to discover what will regain Daddy's attention. One day, Mommy becomes ill. Marcie responds by taking over her mother's functions for the week. Suddenly she is now doing what girls are supposed to do, and Daddy finally responds. Finally Marcie feels she knows how to win once more her father's love and approval. From here on in, Marcie does all the things that girls are supposed to do.

The years pass and the day arrives when Marcie leaves home. And now, every time she meets a man she begins to do things that "girls are supposed to do." The mind makes impoverishing generalities—in Marcie's case her rational mind erroneously equates all men with Daddy. She bakes her man cakes, darns his socks, takes care of his laundry, does his Christmas shopping for him.

One day, a man, overwhelmed by all this attention, believes that he is "in love" with Marcie and asks her to marry him. She has an anxiety attack. Marcie doesn't understand the dynamics of what's happening, but she does recognize that it is time for her to grow as a person. This brings her to an Actualizations Workshop.

In the workshop, Marcie begins to realize that the

way in which she relates to men doesn't allow her any experience of her own value as a person. By behaving towards all men the way she learned she must behave to get her father's "love," Marcie was making it impossible for a real relationship, built on friendship and real love, to develop.

In these conditions Marcie could not experience that she was loved—*even* if she was. Instead, Marcie could only believe that she was wanted for her behavior. So when this man asked her to marry him, Marcie became consumed by the fear of pending enslavement and by the memory of the painful emptiness of her relationship with her father, even when she did succeed in getting his attention and approval. Marcie had no experience of being loved by a man for who she was as a person. She could only conceive of being loved for her behavior.

This impoverished model of male/female relationships leaves Marcie stricken with the fear that if she doesn't continue to behave in her established way, then there won't be any "love" forthcoming. And you know what? There probably won't be, because, given her belief system, Marcie will probably attract a man who views women similarly to her father, who doesn't know how to love, only how to use.

Marcie has set herself up in an impossible "can't win" situation. Her behavior reflects the only choice her impoverished model allows, and this very behavior reinforces her belief in the model.

Here we see our principle at work again. *Every time we act out of fear we keep the fear alive.* We keep reinforcing the fear and imprison ourselves by our own fearful behavior.

Except for her own recognition of her need to seek assistance and grow, Marcie would have spent her life in her prison. That is, unless a miracle occurred. A miracle would look something like this: Marcie meets a man who comes to really care for her and who begins to love her consciously. He recognizes that she holds on to an impoverished model of relationship and says to her: "You know, you don't have to do these things for me. In fact, for a period of three months I forbid you to do these things for me. These months may be difficult for you, but if you see them through, you will discover that it is you that I love, and not just the things you do."

Such miracles are rare. Unfortunately what usually happens in life is that we get only the limited possibilities our impoverished model allows. Consequently we are drawn to somebody who is about where we are, who holds a model of life that complements ours, and together we hold each other's model, and therefore each other, in place.

## Complementary Neuroses

Sadly, so many relationships are built on what I call complementary neuroses. Just as society has its class structure, so does consciousness. We tend to end up with somebody who is currently at about the same level of evolution as we are, unless we have the rare good fortune to meet somebody who can recognize the tremendous reserves of potential that we have, someone who likewise has similar reserves of potential and has actualized much of them and who is now willing to support us in actualizing ours. The relationship will then begin with a degree of inequality, but in a climate of conscious love it can grow to a magnificent equality.

This can happen, but it doesn't happen very often. I would suggest that you do not count on this happening to you. We really do have to see ourselves, and confront and dismantle our own neurotic behavior that comes out of, and at the same time holds in place, our impoverished model of ourselves and of life.

## How to Tell If You Are Neurotic

We are applying the term "neurotic" to any behavior that is based upon the fear of a currently nonexistent problem. For example, the notion that "I'm not good enough" is a nonexistent problem. Any behavior based upon the solution to the problem "I'm not good enough" is neurotic, because, although we may not know it, "I'm not good enough" simply cannot be true, so the problem does not really exist.

Now, it may be a real problem that we do not manifest much of our goodness. Behavior based upon this idea is not necessarily neurotic, because it may be true that we manifest little of our goodness. And if we haven't manifested very much of our goodness and beauty, we had better start working. We can't pay the rent with our potential. We can't use our potential as security on a bank loan.

But if we act out of our fear of inadequacy, out of our feeling of inadequacy we will take action that will effectively reinforce our fear that we are indeed inadequate. In fact, the consequences of our actions will seem to prove that we are inadequate.

In reaction to our—often subconscious—fear, most of us walk around not being real. We are real only when our behavior is appropriately responsive to the moment, rather than an ongoing reaction to past pain and loss, as in the case of Marcie. A real, or highly actualized, person owns his fears and is constantly *responding* in life rather than reacting, so that he resolves his fears. Such a person can express his emotions and feelings honestly. With him, what you see is what you get.

In contrast, most of us walk around in life as a moving violation of the Truth-in-Packaging Act. Indeed, we would be outraged if any product went on the supermarket shelf that was as deceptively labeled as we label ourselves, we would demand reprisals from various consumer-protection agencies. We struggle to

put our act together and take it on the road out of the
fear that we ourselves are not enough. We therefore
struggle to develop an act that other people think is
enough. Hopefully they'll think it's terrific!

Now, this doesn't work in curious ways. The better
the act the worse off we are. The most destructive
thing we can have is a great act. It's curious that a lot
of people who commit suicide have great acts. Most
people around them are absolutely stunned. Because
they were so together.

If you put a really good act together people who
relate at a superficial level will love you. Unfortunately this includes most of the world and so, at a
superficial level, the world will love you. But you will
not feel loved, because you will know that you conned
them with your act. In fact, if your act is successful
enough to elicit for you the adulation and adoration of
tens of thousands of people, you can feel so threatened
by the thought that they might find out that you, "the
emperor," wear no clothes that you will commit suicide. We have seen people in this position do this very
thing. Some of them have been Hollywood stars.

Once we put together this very successful act, we
really have precluded ourselves from having the experience of being admired and loved for ourselves. After
all, if people are telling us they love us and we are
okay, we will instead hear them saying, "I love your
act." We will even find ourselves beginning to despise
the people who tell us they love us and who tell us that
we are terrific. We will despise them for their lack of
perception and for being naïve enough to let themselves be conned by us.

And yet, the fear of not having all that adoration, the
fear of having absolutely nothing at all is so threatening that we just keep on the treadmill until we die or
commit suicide. Once in our own mind we believe that
the love and the respect that people give to us is simply
a result of the act we put together, the longer we
continue with the act the greater and greater grows our

discomfort and sense of emptiness. In some of us this
goes on largely unnoticed and at a subconscious level,
as we head for emotional and physiological disintegra-
tion.

Remember, the act continually reinforces the motivating belief behind the act. The motivation behind the
act is always "I'm not okay." So we feel less and less
okay even though in the viewpoint of the world we are
developing a more and more "successful" life. This is
happening to so many people. There is so much suffering because of this.

Here again we see the conflict between viewpoint
and behavior we discussed earlier. Yes, the act we put
together is gathering the elements of external success,
and in this respect it represents workable behavior.
But because our behavior comes out of an unworkable
viewpoint we do not have the internal experience of
success, and in this respect our behavior is unworkable.

This is why behavior modification by itself doesn't
work. We end up with so-called "workable" behavior
coming out of an unworkable viewpoint. The unworkable viewpoint is the belief and fear that we are not all
right. On top of the unworkable viewpoint, "I'm not
okay," comes the "workable" behavior or act, which
the whole world may applaud. The pressure that we
feel in this double bind can easily become the catalyst
of our own self-destruction.

### How Do I Know I'm Okay?

Workable behavior is only nurturing when it comes
out of the experience that we are already okay. The
next question of course is: "If deep down I don't feel
okay, how can I find out that I am okay?" Obviously
when we don't experience our okayness we can't
come from okayness. We can only pretend and protect. The way to get out of the trap is to stop pretending to be okay and bite the bullet.

When you stop pretending okayness you can begin to discover it. But you have got to stop all activity which is pretense, so that you can begin to build real relationships with people. You may even find out, when you stop the activity that was pretense, that it can actually become real. Because often when we have made that shift in viewpoint, we can once again act just the way we acted before we made the shift in viewpoint. We could say at this point: "I used to be different and now I'm the same!"

Now we are nurtured because our viewpoint and our behavior are in accord rather than conflict. Our life will be an expression of us rather than an attempt to compensate for our erroneous beliefs as we struggle to live in our impoverished model of ourselves.

When we stop our act, many of the people who used to be around us may not be now. But, then again, some will remain and other new friends will appear. Now, however, as we step out from behind our act, we can know that our friends are truly our friends, that they are there because they care for us and not because they are amused by our act. We will now experience that we are indeed lovable and capable.

Love is letting go of fear. Now if somebody says, "I love you," you will know that they do. Now you will have the experience that those who are around you, are around you because of who you are, not because of the way you act, or because of what you have.

This experience is the nucleus of your self-esteem. This is the beginning of the kind of experiences that transform your life. As your behavior begins to flow out of your experience that you are lovable and capable, your whole life begins to shift. While you may go back to doing some of the things you always did, they will now flow from your new experience, of yourself. Now there will be harmony between your viewpoint and your behavior, and you will feel nurtured. You will feel wonderfully alive!

# 7

# On Habits and Depression

### What Is a Habit?

All "bad" habits are a form of avoidance behavior. In other words, the motivating idea behind the habit is an experience we want to avoid. The problem with the habit is that it reinforces the very experience we want to avoid.

The only way out to freedom is for us to discipline ourselves not to indulge in the habitual behavior and to face and resolve the experience we had unconsciously been seeking to avoid. I think that we have pretty well covered this by now. We all have to do our own work. I wish you well.

### What Is Depression?

Depression is habitual inertia. If, for any extended period of time, you cease making an experience of yourself real through action in the world you will become depressed. If we acquire the habit of inactivity, depression is an inevitable companion. Depression is a statement that we are limiting ourselves physically, emotionally, and mentally. Any time we are not expanding we are depressing ourselves.

When we are physically inactive and losing physical energy we are entering a state of physical depression.

When we are losing the experience of love in our life we are entering a state of emotional depression.

If we are losing clarity about our life, we are entering a state of mental depression. If we have questions about our life and no answers, if we feel that we are chasing after our own tails, then we are in a state of mental depression.

### What Is the Cure for Depression?

The total cure for depression is expansion, period. I'll repeat that: *The total cure for depression is expansion.*

The cure for physical depression is physical fitness. While physical depression can be a result of real physical illness that must be appropriately treated by physical means with the assistance of a physician, more often than not, physical depression is simply a lack of physical fitness. Your local bookshop has no shortage of books on the pursuit of physical fitness. This kind of fitness requires your attention to diet, physical rest, and a finely structured exercise program. Diet and exercise are the keys. When these two items of your physical life are balanced, you will inevitably find that you possess more physical energy and require less physical rest than you may be used to.

If you are in any way serious about your personal growth, you must attend to your body and provide it with good nutrition and a balanced exercise program. If you say you are serious about your personal growth and do not do this, you are lying to yourself.

The cure for emotional depression is to find a suitable recipient for your love. This principle and the method of its application are covered in the chapters on Instinctual Love and Conscious Love towards the end of this book.

The lack of physical fitness and particularly the absence of a sound nutritional program can result in difficulties with the body chemistry that can produce emotional depression. There are types of emotional depression that require the assistance of a qualified therapist. But here, again, the total cure for depression is expansion. A competent therapist is really your friendly travel guide and interpreter of reality for the adventure called your life. He cannot do your expanding for you. You alone must do this.

While we may believe that we are emotionally depressed because nobody loves us, this simply isn't true. We are depressed because we are losing the experience of love in our life—not because we are not loved, but because we are not being loving in a way that is received and in a way that is effective. We will leave further discussion about love until later in the book.

The cure for mental depression is the expansion of our minds. As we expand our minds we expand our personal model of reality, enrich our view of the world, and provide ourselves with new choices which, if taken, lead us on to a richer experience of being alive. True education, the purpose of which is the acquisition of wisdom, is a cure for mental depression.

Today's world is filled with rich avenues that will lead us to the expansion of our minds. All they require of us is that we be open, rather than trying to cling to our existing models of reality. If you embrace and use the principles contained in this book you cannot be mentally depressed for any extended period.

Life does have its physical, emotional, and mental ups and downs. These we should simply experience, and we should not try to interfere with this natural cycle. What we are talking about here is being free of the extended periods of contraction or nonexpansion that we call depression.

Remember, expansion is a total cure for depression.

# POWER

# 8

## On Power

"It's still the same old story,
a fight for love and glory . . ."*

If we heed the mythology implicit in the lyrics of this
popular song, it is apparent that life can be fairly
described as the search for the experience of two
things: love and power. "What about money, food,
and sex?" you say. Well, these items are inevitably
regarded (at least subconsciously) as the spoils of
power.

If you are like most people (and, truthfully, virtually
all of us are like most people) you have at least some
attitudes and opinions about power that are negative.
We have all heard the well-cited quote that "power
corrupts and absolute power corrupts absolutely."
Nonsense! This is an idea for the most part peddled by
the seekers of power (who are trying to get it from
those they think have it) to the naïve, the irresponsible, and the fearful, who are never in short supply.

I propose to you a rewrite of this old quote: Weakness corrupts and absolute weakness corrupts absolutely. If you don't like the rewrite too much, it could

---
*"As Time Goes By," words and music by Herman Hupfeld.

be that you have absolute belief in your own powerlessness. We seem wedded to the tragic error that the path to safety is to disenfranchise the powerful and hold the weak blameless for the ills of the world. It would be well for us to remember another old saying, that all it takes for the forces of evil to win in the world is for enough good men to do nothing. The rise to power of Adolf Hitler should serve as a grim reminder of this truth.

During the rise of the Third Reich there was an abundance of evidence that indicated Hitler's real intentions in Europe and his plans for the Jewish people. Well, as Lord Byron pointed out, "hope springs eternal in the human breast." People hoped the stories about the Reich were untrue. They found ways to interpret the available facts to conform to their hopes; never mind the actual reality contained in the facts. The cost was millions of lives. But have we learned anything?

The fact is that power is amoral. It is neither good nor bad. Power is potential; it is, according to Webster, "the ability to act." Nuclear energy is a good example of the amoral nature of power. We can cause the power of the atom to destroy life on this Earth as we know it, or we can use this power to enrich the lives of all people everywhere. The atom, however, has no say in the matter. The atom becomes the tool of our morality. This is a very important principle, one that holds true for all power, so we will say it again: *Power becomes the tool of our morality.* Power becomes the servant of our consciousness.

People with a dark consciousness often feel driven to acquire power, as was the case with Hitler. Be clear, however, that he had the consciousness of darkness long before he persuaded the masses to abdicate their responsibility and hand him their power.

This principle firmly places responsibility for the kind of world we want with each of us as individuals. Even if it runs contrary to your current beliefs and feelings, please heed this: Peace is a product of love, and love is a product of responsible empowerment.

We started with the definition of power as the ability to act, and the next step is to find out where the ability comes from, because if something comes along in life that requires our ability to act, and we feel that we don't have what it takes or know what to do, then the definition alone is not of much use. Power is one thing and results are something else. The ability to act doesn't automatically give us results. We have to take action. The question becomes: Where does the ability to act come from? In answering that question we're going to upset a lot of traditional concepts.

## The Flow of Power—Step One: Clarity

CLARITY, WISDOM, MASTERY, and FACILITY lead to POWER, which enables us to take ACTION, which produces a RESULT, which if CORRECTED, leads to further CLARITY, WISDOM, MASTERY, FACILITY, POWER, ACTION, and RESULTS.

This is the "flow of power."

## Power Starts with Clarity

Clarity simply means that we have a specific image about what we want. Most of us don't have that. Instead, what we've had all our lives are very specific images of what we don't want. Holding images of what we don't want will render us powerless.

Notice that we spend most of our lives trying to be without what we don't want. No power can exist in this context. Even if we succeed in getting free of what we don't want, we will still be without what we do want.

Clarity is a prerequisite for power, clarity about what we want. All the people who get what they want start with, or along the way develop, a very clear picture of what they want.

The kind of power we say we want, which is the power that serves rather than abuses, requires clarity on four levels. The first is clarity at the physical or worldly level. Clarity at this level involves a clear image of what we want in our physical environment and what we want in the way of material possessions.

The second level is clarity of action; in other words, a clear vision of the steps we must take to get the results that we want.

The third level at which we must attain clarity is at the level of thought. This requires true education, which teaches us to think, not to be confused with what often passes for education, which does little else but attempt to fill us full of facts, a task for which computers are better suited.

The fourth and vital level of clarity, if we are to know real power, is clarity of spirit. Clarity of spirit is a function of a clear experience of our relationship with a spiritual reality, otherwise known as God. This is the clarity known as enlightenment.

Under ideal circumstances we begin with clarity of spirit and allow this clarity to flow and illuminate our thoughts, behavior, and acquisitions. This assumes of course that we currently have a clear experience of a spiritual reality. If we don't, we must begin where we are, for any level of clarity is a place to start and is to be preferred to none. Clarity is a habit we must cultivate.

In practical, everyday terms, you must begin with clarity about your desired result. What specifically is it that you want? Describe whatever it is very carefully and in great detail. Ask yourself questions like "Why am I doing this?", "What do I want to accomplish?", "What do I want it to look like?", "How do I want to feel?", "How do I want to be as a person?" The purpose of this questioning is to arrive at a clear vision of what you want. This is the first step.

In the area of material well-being, this means being very specific about our goals: How much money?, What kind of apartment?, What kind of jacket?, What kind of automobile and what color?, How much money can be spent? The visualization of specific results brings clarity to the level of survival. We must be able to handle life at this very basic level, if we are to have the freedom to grow and be fully empowered and alive. We do need to get our logistics together.

Next, we must begin to approach emotional clarity. This allows our empowerment in relationship. Here the question to ask is: "What do I want my experience to be?" (In fact, always ask this question about all aspects of your life, because all goals have as their purpose an implicit assumption about the quality of our experience upon the attainment of the goal.)

In our relationships, we inevitably begin with the wrong kind of clarity and we end up confused about the relationship. We attempt to conduct our relationship using the same kind of clarity we apply to our material existence. We want our lovers to be a certain way. We want them to look a certain way and be a particular size and a particular shape. We want them to dress a certain way and like particular things and to not like particular things. And usually none of our wants reflect any consideration of what they may want. We want them to be our kind of man or woman, rather than their own. Moreover, when they tell us they love us we demand that they tell us our way. We are not content that they say, "I love you," in their own unique way.

When we try to run a relationship using the same rules of clarity we would apply to the game of our material life, it's a mistake. Because relationship is an experiential thing. It is very important that you notice this. If we are going to attain empowerment in the area of relationship, then we must begin with a clarity about our desired experience. As we well know, it is entirely possible to get our relationship to conform to the way we think it should look, only to find it hollow of experience.

And so it is in our emotional and also our spiritual life; clarity can only truly exist and be expressed in experiential terms. In our material or worldly life, clarity can exist and be expressed in terms of specific material things. It is important that we recognize and remember this vital distinction.

Clarity is the beginning of power. On each plane of existence that we seek power, we must first attain the clarity appropriate to that particular plane.

## Wisdom

Let us move on to wisdom. Wisdom is one of the three qualities that traditionally symbolize the attainment of a state of enlightenment. The other two qualities, humor and simplicity, are in fact aspects of wisdom. Humor symbolizes the nonlinear nature of the process of enlightenment. Remember, you cannot get from where you are to laughter through the use of your rational, linear mind, as you discover anytime somebody tries to explain to you a joke you didn't get. It is the nonlinear, intuitive mind, rather than the linear, rational mind, that holds wisdom.

Let us look at what wisdom really is. Wisdom is, quite simply, worldly spirituality. Somebody in an Actualizations Workshop said something that was very elegant. He said: "For a long time I have been concerned with spirituality, in the same way that I saw that most people were concerned with worldliness or materialism. I just realized that Actualizations is about spreading the message of spirituality in practical and worldly terms, and that spirituality and worldliness are companions and not in conflict. That to just be into spirituality is not of service. That to just be into worldliness is not of service. What we need is spirituality in the world."

And this is what wisdom is about: spiritual worldliness.

Wisdom is understanding at an experiential level. It's not the kind of understanding that comes from having learned various facts and having strung them together in an order that makes sense to us, which is what most people mean when they say they understand. What we're talking about here is understanding the nature of existence, the nature of humanity, the nature of relationships, as a result of having had an experience of these things. Only experience can lead to our "knowing" intuitively the conditions that will allow things to work. This is what wisdom is. This kind of knowing brings with it the simplicity inherent in wisdom.

Wisdom requires the kind of understanding Einstein was talking about when he said, "I did not arrive at an understanding of the fundamental nature of the universe through the use of my rational mind." When we're talking about wisdom, we're talking about a level of understanding that is not a product of the rational or linear mind.

We are in no way putting down the rational, linear mind; indeed, it is important. It took the brilliant use of the rational and linear mind to translate Einstein's understanding of the fundamental nature of the universe into the mathematical equations that made it possible to harness the incredible power of the atom. Here we need to note again that power and truth have no inherent virtue. Remember that the first, spectacular use of atomic power was at Hiroshima and Nagasaki. Power and truth have no inherent virtue, but neither do they have inherent evil.

Wisdom is the result of our pursuit of an understanding of the fundamental nature of the universe and what allows life to work in it.

But to say that wisdom is an experiential understanding of the fundamental nature of the universe makes the thought of acquiring it somewhat awesome.

Besides which, the definition is too broad to be practically useful. We must now make this definition useful and no longer awesome, something that we can use every day of our lives.

If we talk of being empowered, for example, in the area of money, then wisdom is an understanding, based on experience, of the laws of money, how to manage it, its real purpose, and the role that money can play in our life. Just as important is an experiential understanding of what money cannot do for us. Money cannot, for instance, buy happiness. Of course, everybody has heard this one. And, of course, almost no one believes that it is true, until they end up with a substantial supply of money, only to find that they are still unable to secure for themselves a happy-ever-after.

If we are talking about being empowered in the area of relationships, wisdom becomes an experiential understanding of the principles that govern creative personal interactions. Here we will require communication skills; we will have to understand the process of letting go of fear and building trust and love.

Be clear that experience does not come out of a book; it can only come out of our full participation in life.

Einstein experienced that what allows the universe to work is the exquisite balance and harmony inherent in the interrelationship of all things that are part of the universe. This can be a delicious experience; it's called enlightenment, or the personal experience of a spiritual reality.

The path to that experience starts with the viewpoint that everything is a series of relationships, that nothing is separate from anything else, that all extremes represent balance. This may be hard for us to recognize.

Perhaps the easiest place of all to begin to look is in the desert, because in the desert, a land of extremes, the delicate balance of nature is exquisitely visible.

There you can see the fundamental nature of the universe at work, and the messages it has for us. Because this world, and everything that is a part of it, truly is our teacher. All the wisdom that you read in the Vedas, in the I Ching, and in the Bible is written in the behavior of the little creatures, the life of the plants, and the balance of the elements of the land. Here we have a school of wisdom.

## Mastery

And now we come to mastery. This is a most beautiful word. It's a word that's traditionally associated with the kind of work this book is about, and it means, really, having acquired a level of excellence in an art, a craft, or a profession. It implies having risen above the complexities of the subject or the activity in which we seek mastery. Mastery comes out of a commitment to excellence. It's a very pragmatic term.

In the broadest sense, a master is one who has risen above the threats, the limitations, and the obstacles of the physical world. A master has control over what we call reality, Or, rather, reality has no power or control over the master. Reality has surrendered to the master. This is the simplest way I can say it. Surrender means to give up possession of and power over. I repeat: Surrender means to give up possession of and power over. So reality no longer holds possession of and power over the master.

This is what being a source is about. When reality has no power over you, does not possess you, then you can be a "source of reality." You say, "Reality will be this way," and it is! That's what being a source is about. Being a source, when you are a human being, means that when you say, "It will be this way," it is! There's nothing esoteric about it. And you may have had that experience without recognizing it.

In New York, in hot weather, when I hail a cab,

seven out of ten times it's air-conditioned. And on occasions when someone says to me, "Do you want me to go and find an air-conditioned cab?" I say, "No, I'll take the first cab that comes along." And we'll get one and the person will be amazed because it will be an air-conditioned cab. I don't take credit for these things. I simply consider them the signals of sourcefulness, an expression of a growing relationship with a spiritual reality. I've had that kind of experience, and you've had it too.

For instance, you think of somebody and the phone rings and that person is on the phone. Or, we walk into our hotel and we have the thought: "I need to get in touch with so-and-so," and there at the front desk will be a message from so-and-so.

It's this kind of seemingly minor event that is an indicator of our being in harmony with the spiritual reality, and it is to be celebrated. This is the easy task, and, of course, there are more important tasks before us. But recognize these little events for what they represent. And remember that mastery is when you say, "Reality will be this way," and it is.

Remember, too, that it is mastery that puts our fear to rest and makes room for the experience of love in our lives and in the world.

Mastery begins with discipline and practice. If you're going to master the piano, or the cello, then you have to devote a great deal of time to practice basic technique. But true mastery, finally, has to be a product of an elevation in our consciousness. The world is full of people who are accomplished technicians who have not graduated as artists. The true artists are people who are somehow larger than their medium.

Pablo Casals was such a human being. I have a recording of the Bach Orchestral Suites, a performance conducted by Casals in celebration of his ninetieth birthday. They are wonderful! The humor, the love and compassion, the spirit and beauty inherent in this collection bring tears to my eyes. They are the work of two masters—Bach and Casals—accomplished beyond most people's ability to perceive the full level of their mastery.

The lesson for us here is that Casals, an artist of exquisite beauty, is so as a result of his own clarity and wisdom regarding the spirit of life itself, in addition to his technical excellence in the field of music. His was not a consciousness limited to music; it was a consciousness that embraced and celebrated life, and it is this consciousness that is reflected in the wonderful readings of those works recorded in celebration of his ninetieth year.

This is a passion for participation in life that leaves the rest of us no place to hide. This is what mastery is about. Sadly, most of us do not do the work at this level, and until we do, we won't have real power.

If you ask enough people to define what a master is, somebody will eventually offer that a master is someone who can perform miracles. This is so. But we had better be clear about what a miracle is. Webster defines a miracle as "a wonderful event, beyond and out of the ordinary" (nothing too esoteric about that!)

In a predominantly negative world, where the average person is treading water in a sea of powerlessness and mediocrity, excellence is a miracle. I have always resonated to the Whirlpool ads proclaiming "excellence is an endangered species." The miraculous path through life is paved by a commitment to excellence. A commitment to excellence begets mastery.

Also, beware that as you go in search of the miraculous, the little people of this world will resent you. Those who have allowed themselves to succumb to mediocrity are likely to begrudge you your miracles, providing of course that they are awake enough to notice.

Mastery demands that we acquire excellence in our chosen field. Think about your profession for a moment. You could be a master in your field, for instance. A master craftsman is a craftsman who produces wonderful results that are beyond and out of the ordinary. A master craftsman is a miracle worker if we accept Webster's definition. In theological literature we find master craftsmen being referred to as among the enlightened. The magnificence of their works was thought to be a miracle, and an expression of the experience of their relationship with God. They were considered to be channels through which the spirit and love of God flowed.

Certainly this was said to be the case with Michelangelo, for example. And there can be no question, if you have ever had the opportunity to gaze upon the extraordinary quality of his work, that here is something wonderful, beyond and out of the ordinary. Truly a miracle by the definition we use.

Thus, mastery begins with a commitment to excellence and craftsmanship. Mastery begins by our being the kind of person who does everything in such a way that we are constantly going beyond our limits. That's what mastery is about. Mastery is a product of consistently going beyond our limits. That means that when somebody else says it's good enough, we say, "No, it isn't." But, again, we should be prepared to encounter some resentment from the little people.

If you are thinking again in very practical terms, look at ways in which you could do what you do at a higher level of excellence. See how you can eradicate mediocrity from your environment and your life.

Look in your automobile glove compartment and trunk. You will probably find that they are a monument to mediocrity, a tribute to sloppiness. Another good place to look is the cupboard under the kitchen sink. Or, what about the food items that may be ready to walk out of your refrigerator? We may laugh about these things, but it is amazing how much stuff we keep around to remind us that mediocrity is acceptable.

Do you want your life to change? Then get everything out of your environment that reminds you that mediocrity is acceptable. Most of us will be living in unfurnished apartments when we get through, although this is very Zen. Take a look at how many things you have around you in your life that support your staying powerless, that support your being average.

So look for all of the things you have around you that support your being a mediocre, or average, little person. Then ask, "Would I be willing to change this? Would I be willing to introduce into my life real changes that are miracles?" True, we are talking about the physical reality, but we have got to start someplace. I see people trying to do it all on the spiritual plane, but if the logistics of day-to-day living are still a hassle, there is no power or mastery at a spiritual level either.

Our life has to be balanced. If you are willing to commit yourself to excellence, to the pursuit of mastery, and to include in your life objects, events, and experiences that reflect the miraculous, your life will change.

If you want to have power, you must have mastery. You can learn from other masters. You may have noticed that masters can be easy to resent, but do you know why? Because they always look like they are on a vacation, while everything they do seems perfect. Life for them seems so easy, and it's easy to resent people like this, because in their presence we can feel like the butt of every joke ever told. A lot of us hang around with idiots, because around an idiot we feel like a genius. In the presence of a master, however, we feel like an idiot with four left feet.

Mastery demands that we give up our resentment of those who have it. This can be tough.

Another thing it takes to acquire mastery is for us to learn to forgive ourselves our klutziness in the presence of a master. We must develop compassion for our own ignorance and lack of skill. Then we can be in the presence of a master and remain open to receive the seed that the experience can plant within us. A seed will not germinate in a compacted, closed soil. Seeds only germinate and grow in open soil.

Can you be as open soil? Can you be as open soil in which the seeds of mastery are planted and nourished and come to fruition? I can't answer that question for you; you have to answer that question for yourself. But I can tell you this, if you don't develop this quality, you are never going to have power.

If you want to remain powerless, just keep saying, "Oh, that's close enough, that'll do." This will keep you powerless. If you want to remain powerless, keep the crowded closets and the appliances that don't work and the clothes that don't fit and the dirty marks on the wall, and this will keep you powerless.

But if you want to have power, and you said you did, then start getting rid of all that stuff. Don't keep things around you that support your mediocrity. Have friends that ask more of you than you do. That will move you along the road to mastery. Don't spend all your time with people you think you are better than. This is a real trap. Risk yourself. What skills could you develop that would allow you to be better at your profession? Discover how you could become a master in your field.

Mastery requires that we rise above the technology of the profession or art form we seek mastery of. Mastery is beyond technique. It starts with technique, but it goes beyond technique. If you are still struggling with technique, then you had better keep at it until you are beyond it. Because mastery is revealed when you are no longer inhibited by a struggle with the technology and techniques of your art form. When the techniques and technology of your art form no longer confine or inhibit you but are simply a channel through which your spirit flows to become real in the world, then you have found mastery.

### Facility

The next item in the flow of power is facility. Facility is the term we use to describe the physical, emotional, mental, and spiritual means by which something can be done. For instance, if you want to be a cellist, you first need the facility of the physical use of a cello. You need the facility of a teacher who has some mastery in the technology of playing the cello. As a performer, you will need the facility of an audience. Finally, you will need the facility of inspiration to truly communicate the spirit of your music.

Ask yourself what facilities you have, or need to have, in order for you to attain your goals. Money, for instance, is a facility. People who will participate with you and support you in what you want to accomplish are a facility. Your own energy, ideas, and commitment to your goals are facilities. Your home, your car, your possessions are facilities. If you run a business, your staff is a facility.

### This Is Very Important: Facility Is Not Reward

I know that many of us make the error of seeing a facility as a reward, as a goal in itself. For instance, we have come to view money, houses, cars, and beautiful possessions as rewards. In fact, some of us see love or support as a reward for being nice or being good. It's generally true in our society that wages, fringe benefits, vacations, pension benefits, etc., are all presented as rewards for getting the job done. But these things, when properly understood, will no longer be viewed as rewards. They are the facilities, or means, by which we are able to get the job done in life.

For example, it's hard to play football unless we have a team, uniforms, a field, goalposts, and a ball. We don't see these things as rewards, but if we don't have them it's hard to play the game. In the same way, if we don't have money, it's hard to play life. If we don't have food and a place to live, it's hard to play. The things we hold as rewards are really facilities which allow us to play in the game and accomplish our goals.

As an employer, it's a mistake to offer people rewards if we want them to be powerful. We must learn to recognize that we give people salaries as a facility, so that they have the means by which they can accomplish more in their profession and life. Their level of facility should match their level of ability to use the facility wisely and productively.

You will regard your possessions as facilities, rather than rewards, when you are no longer attracted to owning them, and when your only interest is in having the use of them. When you view your possessions as rewards, they disempower you. This also holds true when you feel that you need them as proof that you're all right, or as a demonstration to the world that you are success, or as a security against the future.

I've noticed that many of us have trouble in giving ourselves permission to have beautiful things, because we consider that on some level we are not worthy of such rewards. I promise you that all the guilt and discomfort you experience because you think you don't deserve what you possess, or desire to possess, will disappear when you begin to regard these things as a facility. As a facility, they will empower you and enable you to participate joyfully in life, and enable you to effectively support other people in their participation in life.

I know a lot of us think we only deserve to have nurturing relationships when we're in good shape, when we're happy and feeling good, when we think somehow we've done something to deserve them. We think that when we're tired or grumpy or things aren't going well at work we don't deserve love and support. When we don't like ourselves very much we tend to be uncomfortable about other people liking us. We have difficulty letting people love us because we think we have to deserve it.

Love is a facility and is to be treasured as such. If somebody wants to love you, recognize that—whether or not you think you're worth it—it's an enormous contribution to that person to allow yourself to receive his or her love. It's often a great struggle to allow someone to love you. If you're around a loving person, let that person love you whether you think you deserve it or not, because in so doing you are also being of service to him or her. It's really so simple. Loving people is easy; it's getting to accept love that is difficult. We are empowered when we offer love and it is received. In this way we make a difference.

## How to Empower Yourself and Others

I want to talk a bit more about facility, about what to do to empower, rather than disempower, yourself and others.

First, acknowledge the facility that you already have. Take the time to sit down and look at your own level of clarity, your own wisdom, your own resources, and acknowledge them for all that they are. The most powerful facility you can have is by being the kind of person who is willing to support others and who is willing to allow others to support you.

*All facility comes from your ability to have relationships that work.* And this takes acknowledgment of yourself and other people, and it takes being open to being supported, as well as your willingness to give support and contribution.

Think of money, material abundance, love, and the experience of a relationship with spiritual reality as a facility. This is a very important principle.

A facility only becomes valuable when it is used consciously and with good purpose. Truly powerful people have great abundance of facility, which they consciously use with good purpose. It is their wise use of facility that enables them to make a positive difference in the world.

In fact, if you are a person of integrity, the only way you can have abundance and be nurtured is to regard it as a facility. I know a lot of you feel that abundance is incompatible with integrity. And it is, if you regard abundance as a reward, because to regard it as a reward is to deny a spirit of service that must come to exist in the world. To regard abundance as a facility is a context within which to hold abundance, a context which can change the face of the world, because it carries with it the spirit of service.

## Results

By now we're beginning to see the principle from which power flows. We've looked at four very important items which determine our ability to act. The next step in this flow of power is to take action.

*Results require action.* This is the time to set aside our fear. Results are the consequence of taking action. Only action can make facility valuable. If we don't take action, there aren't any results. Many of us try to avoid this step but it cannot be avoided if we want results. The absence of workable action is the major cause of all failure. If we don't take action that comes out of clarity, wisdom, and mastery, action that is supported by facility, we will be ineffective and our results, if any, in life will be unsatisfactory. *Read this paragraph at least three times.*

## Correction

Regardless of the quality of the result, it's important that you notice the result and acknowledge yourself as being responsible for it. This next step is very important. Examine your result and begin to make all possible corrections. The better the result, the more valuable correction becomes as a form of fine tuning. It's much easier to find a speck of dust on a white wall than to find a white wall under a pile of garbage, but the first step may have to be cleaning up the garbage so we can see that the wall exists.

We seem to have a fear of interacting with reality, a fear of going forward and actually producing results in the real world. This fear has been lumped loosely into the category called "fear of failure." But that doesn't tell us anything. Fear of failure is really the fear of being wrong that we have examined in some detail.

I have received a marvelous education in this whole subject of results and correction on an airplane ride to Hawaii. The captain of this Boeing 747 happened to be a friend of mine, and after we were airborne he invited me up to the flight deck to ride in his chair. Except for the landing, when I had to return to my own seat, I stayed in his chair for the entire flight.

Between the chair in which I was sitting and the chair where the copilot was sitting was a cosole supporting a tray of doughnuts and coffee. I thought this was its only purpose. The captain, whose name was Chuck, saw me looking at the console. "You want to see what's inside there?" he asked. I told him yes, and he opened it up. Inside was a little black box.

"It's the inertial navigation system," he said. "It tells us where we are. In the days of propeller-driven aircraft, we used to have human navigators. Then we started flying DC8's, which went at nearly the speed of sound, and that became a problem. By the time a human navigator would work out where we were, we weren't there anymore. So we had to come up with a better system.

"This little black box tells us exactly where we are with almost zero time delay. It simply tells us where we are without deciding that it's a good or a bad place to be. Where we are is where we are. Therefore, it can't be unhappy—you have to decide that where you are is bad in order to be unhappy. The little box always knows exactly where we are coming from, and it knows whether where we are is where we said we'd be in the flight plan. If there is a discrepancy, it lets us know exactly what correction to make.

"This little black box," he continued, "literally uses

the universe as a guru. It uses the universe as a source of wisdom about our position, because it plots our position relative to the other planets. It does not plot our position by looking into itself. It calculates where we are by looking outward at the world."

I said, "This is a marvelous analogy for people, because most of us try to figure out where we are by looking inside our heads."

"Yes," he said, "and therein lies a problem. This little black box will get us to within one thousand yards of the runway in Honolulu. It could get us within one thousand yards of a runway on the moon if we could fly to the moon. And this is only the beginning.

"I notice that you talk about people's reluctance to take action. They have a fear of being foolish and are unwilling to be in error or to be caught in error, and they have great sensitivity about being corrected.

"The fascinating fact is that we are going to touch down on the runway in Hawaii within five minutes of our estimated arrival time when we left. We will arrive in Hawaii almost precisely on time, having been in error during 90 percent of the trip.

"It is most important that we realize this. A rocket to the moon spends 90 percent of its time in error. If we could accept that we can get a rocket to the moon and a 747 to Honolulu that have been in error 90 percent of the time, we might be a little less uptight about being in error ourselves."

I was loving this conversation and remembered that a sailboat traveling into the wind cannot get from where it is to where it wants to be by traveling in a straight line. It has to zigzag. So, in terms of its destination, its course is always in error. What is important about the sailboat, the rocket, and the 747 is that the errors are corrected.

So the path from here to where we want to be starts with an action that contains an error, which we correct, which becomes the next error, which we correct, which becomes the next error, which we correct, and that becomes the next error which we correct. So the only time we are literally on course is that moment in the zig-zag when we actually intersect our direct path. The rest of the time, we are in error.

It appears to be a closely guarded secret that excellence is the product of extensive correction. I sense that this idea is foreign to many of us. However, if you will look at the areas in your life where you are at your best, you will discover that these areas of excellence are the result of a great deal of practice, a great deal of trial and error, and a lot of correction. The process of correction is essential to power. Without correction there is no enhancement of our clarity, we do not grow in wisdom, there is no progress towards mastery and there is a dissipation of facility, with impoverishing consequences.

It was during the airplane ride that I began to see how sensitive we all are to being corrected, and how the way we respond to being corrected is a reflection of our own self-esteem. I found myself imagining times that I'd been asked out to dinner. And I imagined that a lady had asked me to dinner and was going to cook cannelloni at her place.

I arrived at the appointed hour on the appointed day clutching red roses and a fine wine, and we go through the pleasantries that people go through, and then we sit down when dinner is served.

The lady says to me, "Stewart, how's the cannelloni?" And I respond, "Well, it's great. I think that you make terrific cannelloni, and that probably you could join the ranks of the cannelloni maestros of the world—if, the next time you make this dish, you add half a glass of dry white wine and a tablespoon of fresh, chopped sweet basil to the sauce two minutes before you take it from the heat."

I speculated that what may very well happen next is that I may find myself wearing cannelloni.

There are two possibilities here. Possibility number one is that I don't know the first thing about cannelloni. In fact, I could be so ignorant in culinary matters that I don't know the difference between cannelloni and a burrito. In which case, this lady has become upset in response to the input of a fool. That places her in an area of even greater foolishness than this fool who gave her the input.

At the other extreme, the possibility is that I am one of the great culinary experts in the world. In which case, to be upset by input that was accurate, supportive, and that, in fact, would elevate her to the ranks of the cannelloni maestros of the world would be inappropriate.

It is interesting that no matter what our response is to correction, any response that takes offense or reflects an upset is inappropriate, no matter what position the person who offers the correction is taking. If the person who gives us the correction is a fool, to be upset by a fool is to make ourselves an even greater fool. If the input is of great value, to not consider it places us once again in the category of the fool.

So if we respond negatively to feedback, it is a reflection of our own foolishness and a reflection of our own absence of self-esteem in this area of our life.

I told this story to Chuck, who, getting very excited, said, "Well, I've got to introduce you to somebody else in the plane." And the somebody else was the autopilot. Now, they call the inertial navigation system Fred, and the autopilot they call George. And we began to examine the relationship between Fred and George.

Their relationship in engineering terms is called a closed-loop feedback mechanism, which is just a fancy way of saying that Fred and George never get out of communication, that they always supply each other with feedback, they don't make each other wrong, and they don't take anything personally.

All the way to Hawaii, Fred and George have this conversation. Fred will say, "George, we're off course two degrees to starboard." And George will say, "Okay, Fred, I'll fix it."

"George, we're off course three degrees to port."

"Okay, Fred, I'll fix it."

"George, we're Dutch rolling."

"Okay, Fred, I'll fix it."

"George, we're twenty knots below our optimum air speed."

"Okay, Fred, I'll fix it."

"George, we're one hundred feet below our allocated air corridor."

"Okay, Fred, I'll fix it."

And this conversation goes on all the way to Hawaii. Now, if Fred and George happened to be human beings instead of technology, the conversation would probably go something like this:

"George, we are off course two degrees to starboard."

"Okay, Fred, I'll fix it."

"George, we're off course three degrees to port."

Pause. "Okay, Fred, I'll fix it."

"George, we're Dutch rolling."

"All right, Fred, I'll fix it."

"George, we're forty knots below our right airspeed."

"Oh, for God's sake, Fred! Bitch, bitch, bitch! All you ever do is bitch!"

Two ordinary people would take this all very personally. Yet this feedback and correction is the essence of the relationship that allows the safe arrival of the airplane in Hawaii.

It is the correction of each result in our life that leads to an increase in our clarity, wisdom, mastery, and facility, which in turn elevates us to the next level of power, enhances our ability to act, and ensures a higher level of results, providing for the enrichment of our lives.

On the old TV series "Star Trek" they have a marvelous system of red alerts and yellow alerts. The yellow alert means things are about to be not good and we'd better do something. If we don't do something, then there is a red alert, which means things are definitely going to get very bad very fast, and if we don't get it together, we are going to be blown into interstellar space by a Klingon battle cruiser. Of course, Captain Kirk and Mr. Spock do get it together and it all turns out—until the next rerun.

As I looked in my own life and at the lives of the people I've worked with, I recognized that there are always yellow alerts and red alerts out there for us. They let us know how we're doing. If we look, we will see that there are little flags, little signposts, little alerts that say, "Hey, wait a minute, maybe you are off course," or "Wait a minute, maybe you ought to take a look and correct." This taught me something very basic about failure.

Failure, for the most part, is not a result of our lack of ability, but a consequence of our basic lack of attention to the yellow and red alerts that light up in life, and our failure to correct the errors as they are revealed.

We are fundamentally no different from the 747 on its way to Hawaii or the rocket on its way to the moon. To be in life means that we are constantly off course. What is important is not that we are off course but whether or not we make the corrections that need to be made.

I see that most of us don't make the necessary corrections because we are too busy protecting ourselves. Most of our failures in life are a consequence of protecting ourselves when we should have been correcting ourselves.

The unwillingness to be in error and to correct is the source of most misery.

Powerful people are like the 747 and the rocket. They are willing to be in error and they are willing to correct. They are people who are busily doing what they don't know for sure how to do. That's the adventure for them. They don't know what's around the next corner. They do know that they are committed to a path of spiritual, mental, emotional, physiological, and material growth. They know they will do whatever has to be done when they get around the next corner so they can get around the corner that's around the next corner.

To have power we must have access to the spiritual, mental, emotional, physiological, and material elements of power. True power demands this balance of facility, and we alone are responsible for discovering our own path of access to these facilities. While undoubtedly there is such a thing as inequality of opportunity, the fact remains that each of us has before us more opportunity than we will ever reach for. So start stretching!

To regain our power we must now come to recognize the kinds of facility that will support us beyond the impoverishment of our own personal model of reality. Having made this discovery we must next place ourselves in the midst of this support and begin to *act courageously*. Remember, *courage is taking creative action in the presence of fear*.

## In Review: Why Don't We Have Power?

What is it beyond fear that prevents us from having an experience that we are powerful, loving, and effective people?

First, the belief in ideas that impoverish our personal model of reality; these ideas do not support our experience of being a loving and effective person. We have looked at some of these ideas, we've seen where many of them come from, what kinds of people they came from. And so it should be no surprise to us that, given the people who sold us these ideas, we, believing them, have no experience of ourselves as powerful, loving, or effective people. The people who sold us these ideas did not have much, if any, experience of themselves as loving or effective people, and if they at times experienced a sense of power, it was the kind of power one has over people who are too irresponsible or too naïve or too frightened to resist the control of even a well-intentioned oppressor.

What kind of satisfaction does anyone really find in that sort of power? The evil scientist who threatens to blow up the world is caught between two unpleasant choices: to annihilate himself as well as the rest of humanity when he throws the switch or, if he has managed to secure some kind of haven for himself, to survive alone without the company of his own kind. The power that oppresses is not real power, it is the "fight" reaction to fear, manifested over a period of time.

In our own lives perhaps the greatest impediment to our own power is the surrender of our belief in our personal power to people or institutions that don't necessarily support our well-being. This is really a statement that we surrender our belief in ourselves, because we don't really ever surrender our power. We do not, after all, lose our ability to act, until we die. We lose our *belief* in our ability. And this is important, because this belief can be regained by recognizing what we have done.

## The Cult of the Victim

I've noticed a curious thing about the way we give up our power to others. We tend to give up our power more readily to people who are aggressive. We don't often give up our power to people we perceive to be wiser than ourselves, gentler than ourselves, more compassionate than ourselves, or more loving than ourselves; wherein we may have gained something of value, including power itself.

Most of us give up our power to people who will treat us badly, and we organize our lives around these people. We vote for them, marry them, and go to work for them. If we succeed in impeaching them, moving out, or getting away, and starting life over, we very often find another person of the same type with whom to replace the one we just left.

Beyond this, we seem dedicated to making ourselves vulnerable to continual assault by people who treat us with hostility and condescension, and we seem unwilling to surrender to those people who do love and support us. Remember, the word surrender means to give up possession of, or control over.

## Love Is a Weakness, We Think

This is because we have constructed an impoverished model of reality in which we see love as weakness. We think love is the opposite of power. Dissatisfaction, conflict, and unhappiness are the price we pay for this impoverished model of reality.

As we give up our personal power, we start comparing ourselves to the standards we think are held by those we've given our power to. And we will never meet those standards, whether real or imagined. Some of us are so dedicated to unhappiness through self-condemnation that we no longer need someone else to treat us badly. We learn to treat ourselves badly. In fact, there are those among us who arrange for our own very real physical suffering in propitiation of our imagined sins and shortcomings.

What did we hope to gain by giving up our belief in ourselves? The hope that someone else would believe in us and would approve of us.

## We Trade Power for Love, and It's a Lousy Deal

For the most part we have relinquished our power in the name of "love" (read "approval"). In the hope of being loved by someone, whether it be our parents, our spouse, our friends, our employer, or our country, we have surrendered our power and/or our belief in our power. All this is in deference to institutions and relationships that do not necessarily have our best interests at heart, or whose interests are unrelated to our happiness.

And as long as we give away our power, we won't have any. As long as we give away our power, we will not make a positive difference anywhere, either in our own lives or in the lives of others.

## The Validity of Our Own Experience

What is it that we are giving up every day that we don't claim for ourselves our own power? We are giving up the validity of our experience. More than that, we are giving up the validity of our experience to a myth—to something that is either crazy or untrue and which does not support a happy and productive life.

We—against all evidence—hope that the people we have placed in authority above us, the heroes we have made into our saviors, those to whom we have given our power, will somehow take responsibility for the misery in our lives, will solve our problems for us, will tell us the right thing to do, will save us from our suffering, and most of all will tell us we aren't as bad as we think we are. We demand of our heroes that they lead us out of the wilderness of our experience. We give them our power and create the lie that they, rather than us, are responsible for our life. This way we have someone to blame, and it isn't us.

Enough of this nonsense! It is time to reconstruct our model of reality and reclaim our power!

# 9

## On Sex

### Sex: The Shame and Glory of Humanity

It used to be that sex was dirty. Then along came the so-called Sexual Revolution, and we thought that sex was now going to be okay. But unfortunately we have only succeeded in making it okay for sex to be dirty.

With all of our openness, all of our frank and honest conversations about our sexuality, has anything really changed? Or are we merely on one end of a pendulum that has been swinging back and forth for centuries?

Why do we experience so much conflict about an activity so fundamentally a part of life? Many of us know that sex can be one of life's greatest pleasures. And in this may lie part of the answer. At least some of the conflict surrounding human sexuality is a carry-over from the inherited conflict over the experience of pleasure itself. It may be that we have simply become unable to allow ourselves to have the experience of pleasure. We have therefore developed a subconscious need to deny ourselves the pleasure of sex, thereby making it an issue.

No one can argue that sex for the most part has become an issue rather than a pleasure. But what if sex for us was a pleasure instead of an issue—a medium of expression, a channel of pure communication between us and an expression of our love for one another? What if sex was what it could be, what it is only rarely?

For us to be able to look at sex sanely, we first need to examine the roots of our insanity about it. We need to explore the conflicting customs, ideals, and mythologies that we have inherited as our model of sexual reality.

Our attitudes about sex today are a conglomeration of twenty or more centuries of conflicting attitudes which in various forms have been handed down to us and have become part of the way we think. By now we are more and more used to the notions that we have been taught and have internalized these contradictory points of view. We struggle to resolve these contradictions often without even recognizing that they are contradictions. Modern marriage is probably the most significant manifestation of this attempt.

## Our Sexual History

To understand our present attitudes about sex we need to study the history of the development of these attitudes.

Sex is a major preoccupation in our culture, if our newspapers, movies, television shows, novels, and magazines are an accurate barometer. Moreover, we humans are the only creatures who have found it necessary to deliberately inhibit the sex drive. And, if sex is a major preoccupation, it is also the activity which has been subject to the greatest regulation over the ages, both public and private. The history of what we call our civilization reveals an unending conflict between our powerful and supposedly dangerous sex drive and the various systems of suppression which have been established to control it.

Given our past, it is no wonder that our present-day sexual attitudes are sometimes grotesque and often irrational. They are actually a hodgepodge of customs and regulations, from pre-Christian and early non-Christian societies and religions, from the Christian ascetic tradition as it developed over the last two thousand years, and from the Romantic tradition as it was developed in the Middle Ages and as it was revived and revised by the nineteenth-century Romantic poets.

Regardless of what we may have been taught in our social science classes, sex is more than a biological urge. In many societies it has been traditionally associated with creativity and with the attainment of heightened states of consciousness.

Before the Christian era, sex was, together with religion, one of the two principal paths into the unconscious. Often the two were combined. With the establishment of the Christian Church, the path of sex became almost entirely closed and the path of religion became heavily policed. Sex has been an instrument of lovers and sadists alike, and it has been linked with violence to an uncomfortable degree.

Our attitudes about sexual matters affect and even dictate our attitudes towards social and other matters. And these attitudes are often subjective and individual as well as officially prescribed by the legal or spiritual authorities.

## Our Morals Are Subject to Change Without Notice

Our attitudes towards sex are subject to change. The word "moral," in fact, comes from the word *mores*, which means customs. What is moral, then, is what is customary, what we are accustomed to, and what we are accustomed to is subject to change, often in the most surprising ways.

At any time, our own private code of sexual conduct may or may not be in accord with the currently approved way of behaving. The conflicts about sex that develop in us have as much to do with the discrepancy we perceive between our actions and personal beliefs as they do with the actual discrepancy between our private beliefs and the sexual reality of our society. It is our behavior that is inconsistent with what we *believe* is correct that is most likely to result in our feelings of guilt and shame, as opposed to behavior that is not sanctioned by law or blessed with public approval.

## Alternate Models: Ancient Sparta and Athens

Sexual matters in early Greece and Rome were treated with an openness which has only been present in Europe during a very few periods. The social structure of the Greeks seems to have bred little frustration. In classical Greece sexual codes were established by the civil authorities, rather than by the religious authorities. Celibacy, far from being a virtue, was forbidden! Rape was a crime. Virginity was important as a factor in a young woman's marriageability but it was not considered a virtue in and of itself.

There was no prohibition of public nudity for either men or women. Prostitution was legal, and prostitutes were not social outcasts. Usually they were associated with the temple of a particular goddess. In general, these women, known as hetaerae or courtesans, were more educated than their married sisters, had more freedom, and in many cases were welcome in the best society.

Sexual habits were therefore left largely to taste and custom. The Greeks accepted homosexuality with little comment. They recognized that the sexual nature of every human being contains both homosexual and heterosexual elements.

They also recognized the need of individuals to release sexual tension as well as aggressive tendencies, and the cult of Dionysus, which we may think of today as an excuse for unlicensed sex, was a social device for the release of such tensions. In a sense, it was an institutionalized outlet for people's lust.

Dionysus, by the way, who is these days promoted as the god of wine, was originally associated with psychedelic mushrooms, particularly the smooth and delightful Psilocybe, which is enjoying a renaissance of popularity in our day and age. Unfortunately for Western humanity, Dionysus was purged of his association with magic mushrooms and was pronounced the god of wine. The Church and the state much preferred the masses to use alcohol, which suppresses consciousness, rather than mushrooms, which illuminate it.

The Greeks looked with special interest on any process that seemed able to induce an awareness of divinity. They knew that music, dancing, and mushrooms could cause it, and found it to be present also at the climax of the sexual union, where the bounds of our personality seem to dissolve and we merge with the infinite.

The Greeks saw in the creative power of sex not only a vitally important force, upon which humanity, and indeed all life, depended, but also a positive miracle. It was the one solid reason for optimism in a world which must have seemed to them as dangerous and destructive as our own. This point of view, as we will see, is antithetical to the one put forth in the Middle Ages by the Roman Catholic Church, the one that forms the basis, consciously or unconsciously, for most of the sexual attitudes we hold today.

Be clear that the modern Church does not accurately reflect the custom or spirit of the early Christians and that there is little in the source books from that time that would lead us to anticipate the extremes to which the medieval Church carried its repressive sexual policies.

There is nothing in the literature of the early Christians to indicate that they thought sex was sinful. Celibacy may have been a virtue, but it was considered a special gift from God, which only a few received. Women participated fully in the religious and social life of the group. They could serve as preachers and healers who baptized as well as exorcised.

The early Christians apparently existed in numerous small communities which were held together by a very real and vivid experience of their religion. They practiced a kind of brotherly love which is most usually described by the Greek word *agape*, used to denote an unattached, nonpossessive, brotherly/sisterly quality of love. Religious belief was not important to them. They were Christians not by belief but by practice. They did not celebrate either the birth or the death of Christ as festivals, nor the Holy Communion as we now know it. They did not claim that Christ was divine or that he was born of a virgin.

They celebrated what they called the Agape, a meal in which real food was shared, and which was the occasion for prayers, inspired conversation, and the evocation of the mystical. The Agape they regarded as the central and essential feature of their religion.

Early Christianity seems to have been a movement based, in a quite literal sense, on love. They lived together in groups in order to experience love deeply, to explore the potential within each of them to feel and express love, regardless of sex, individually and as a group. In short, the characteristic of early Christianity seems to have been the existence of loving groups in which sex distinctions were forgotten and whose *raison d'être* was a genuine religious experience.

## What Went Wrong, and When

The transformation of this religion into what it has become today began in the third and fourth centuries after Christ. The first step was to replace the Agape with the Holy Communion. This was done in stages. The effect of the change was most significantly the shift from the group experience to the individual experience. The consequences of this shift were several.

The relationship of God to man became individual;
worship and meditation became private instead of
communal; and the believer became individually responsible to a priest, who became his go-between with
God. There was no longer a shared and communal
religious experience. The Church now owned the individual.

As the living religious experience was squeezed out
of Christianity, it became necessary to substitute
something. The substitutes found were masochistic
self-torture, and the creation of an elaborate body of
doctrine. *The criterion of being a Christian ceased to
be the ability to experience a certain change in oneself, and to manifest love as a result, and became the
willingness to believe in certain doctrines.*

## The Rise of the Devil, Flagellation and the Cult of the Devil

Included in the creation of doctrines was the establishment of Christ's divinity from the moment of conception instead of from the time of his baptism, the
creation of the Nativity as a major feast, and the
change of his birth date from early autumn to Decem-
ber 25 (the date of a major pagan feast). Together with
these there developed an ecclesiastical hierarchy, a
depression in the status of women, and the beginning
of a profound intolerance for people whose religious
beliefs were not in accord with the current dogma of
the Church.

The first persecutions were against Mithraism, a
pagan religion which was abused with great ferocity
and then absorbed to a great degree by the Church.
This is the beginning of a habit by the Church to
destroy heresies with great vengeance and at the same
time or shortly thereafter incorporate those same heresies into the dogma of the Church. Flagellation, the
cult of the Virgin Mary, and the rise in the importance

of the Devil as an enemy of God are a few examples of this.

## Goodbye Belief, Hello Doctrine

In any case, what is significant about the development of the Christian movement is the rejection of the early doctrine (and later heretical doctrines) of "justification by works" in favor of "justification by faith," the latter being the belief in the truth of certain propositions. There was, in addition, an unwillingness on the part of most Christian faiths to allow a man to call himself a Christian because he behaved in an honorable and kindly manner.

Indeed, to the contrary, the major religions have usually persecuted such people when they did not subscribe to all the articles of the official Christian model of reality.

The Romans did not ordinarily persecute people for their religious beliefs, but they made an exception in the case of the Christians because they were horrified by the intolerance and fanaticism that the Christians developed, as well as by their readiness to justify the most appalling means by the end they desired to attain. The Romans felt the Christians threatened the whole established order, as they indeed turned out to do. Emperor Marcus Aurelius (ruled A.D. 161–200), a very rational and moral man, considered Christianity to be immoral.

## The Permissive Culture of the Early Middle Ages

If we turn to England in the early Middle Ages (A.D. 800–1000), we find a people who maintained a free sexual morality. Most people thought sexual abstinence was unhealthy. Prostitution was widespread and supported by the authorities. A state of public nudity to the degree found on bathing beaches today was acceptable, and many towns had public baths.

Marriage was a private and often temporary affair. Women were free to take lovers before and after marriage, and men were free to seduce all women of lower rank and to attempt to win the favors of women of equal and higher rank by feats of bravery.

Women enjoyed a good deal of freedom, although there is some indication that a married woman was in some sense the property of her husband. In any case, the Celts are considered to have had a permissive society and were thought to be a people who did not impose their views on others.

To be called a bastard in this society was not a mark of shame but one of distinction, since the implication was that one's mother has had an affair with some especially valiant knight, who was therefore one's father. It was into this society that the Catholic missionaries came.

### Enter the Missionaries (and Other Knights of the Order of the Wet Blanket)

It was several centuries before the missionaries succeeded in instilling their sexual codes on these people, for it was necessary to somehow get people to accept codes that were greatly at odds with the ones they presently enjoyed.

The indoctrination was carried out on many fronts. First, as has been mentioned before, the biblical records were distorted and falsified to support the new model of reality being presented to the people. Passages were taken out of context to support celibacy, the prohibition of masturbation, and various other things. Self-denial was not given anywhere near the importance in the Bible that it was given by the medieval Church.

The old folktales were also rewritten. King Arthur and his knights, for instance, were represented in the new versions of the stories as paragons of chaste and gentlemanly behavior. In the Christianized versions of these tales, the king offers his daughter's hand in marriage to the knight who slays the dragon or otherwise saves the kingdom, but in the original versions marriage does not enter the picture, just a one-night stand!

In the earliest Celtic versions of the Tristan story, in fact, Tristan is simply a hero with whom Iseult has an affair before she marries King Mark, and, given the morality of the times, this was a perfectly unremarkable event.

What we find in the older tales, then, is not immorality, but a different set of rules, a set of rules which has become greatly at odds with the Christian model of reality. The willing—or unwilling—seduction of men and women was not immoral behavior to the people the Christian missionaries encountered in England, but part of a tradition, a system of sexual mores that had been in existence long before the arrival of the missionaries and that continued to exist for many hundreds of years thereafter.

Another way the new sexual codes were imposed was through increasingly strict rules for the clergy. The role of women as preachers and healers was diminished and eventually vanished. It was with great difficulty that priests were banned from marrying. There are instances of priests murdering their abbots for preaching better behavior to them, or leaving their endowed Church office to their sons in open defiance of a rule forbidding that.

The clergy were strongly opposed to the rule of celibacy. They married in defiance of the prohibition, or contented themselves with sexual adventures among the female parishioners, or with homosexuality. There were instances of parishioners insisting their priest have a mistress as a measure of protection for their wives. It was said that in many towns the number of illegitimate offspring outnumbered those children born in wedlock, and in Germany the word for parson's child was used as a synonym for bastard.

So the agents upon whom the Church depended to uphold its sexual codes were as unwilling as anyone else to live under them. And the nature of the power the priests had over their congregation led to widespread abuse of all kinds.

## Sexual Taboos of the Dark Ages, or No Wonder We Can't Have a Good Time Today

Let's take a look at some of the sexual taboos that were imposed by the Church in the Middle Ages, for it is from these taboos that European and American sexual ideals have been primarily derived. These sins were drawn up in elaborate detail in books employed by the priests, who used them as guides during confession to determine the precise nature of the wrongdoing of those seeking absolution.

The Church's ideal model of sexual behavior was embodied in an elaborate code of regulations which was based upon the conviction that the sexual act was to be avoided like the plague, except for the bare minimum necessary to keep the race in existence, and even when performed for this purpose, it remained a regrettable necessity.

The following were declared to be sins, in addition to the general prohibition above:

1) sex between unmarried people
2) adultery
3) kissing
4) thinking of sex
5) nocturnal emissions
6) homosexuality
7) masturbation
8) all coital positions other than the "missionary" position
9) having sex on other than prescribed days, and the days on which sex was forbidden included the following: Sundays, Wednesdays, Fridays,

forty days before Easter, forty days before Christmas, and from the day of conception until forty days after the child was born
10) desire (even for one's husband or wife)
11) any pleasure experienced (still official doctrine today)

Also forbidden were dancing, horse racing, and theater. Both the general conception of sex as sinful and many of the specific prohibitions have survived almost intact up to the present and still affect our behavior. Some of the prohibitions became civil law and as such remain on some of our statute books to this day.

It is very important that we notice the general prohibition of pleasure in all forms. This was even more suppressive than the incredible restrictions on sexual activity. It was the acceptance of this idea, more than the belief in the rightness of any particular sexual regulation, which allowed the Church to have the power over people that it did. For only if a person came to believe that pleasure was a sin could he be depended upon to manufacture his own sense of guilt and wrongdoing.

The Church's fear of sex was fundamentally superstitious. It preserved the primitive magical belief in the power of sex to contaminate, which the Celts also shared to some extent. One consequence of belief in the power of sex to contaminate was the degradation of women. If men in the Celtic society had certain rights of property in their wives, the prejudice of the Church made this inequality insignificant. The Church regarded woman as the source of all sexual evil. She was the temptress, and in matters of sexual misconduct, she was considered to blame.

By the twelfth century the sexual dictates of the Church had acquired a considerable hold on the lives of the people of England. The Anglo-Saxon Church placed more emphasis upon the regulation of sexual activity than probably any other general code of conduct.

The Church had discovered that no physical system of supervision could hope to regulate the most private acts and thoughts of men. Only a system of psychological control based on terror would serve.

## Pleasure Becomes a Capital Offense

Let's look at the results of the Church's actions, for they became the building blocks of our impoverished sexual reality. As soon as people internalized these restrictions, the result for many was the manifestation of behavior we would today call neurotic, or perhaps psychotic. Whenever a society attempts to restrict the expression of human sexuality more severely than our constitution will stand, either people will defy the taboos, as they often did, turn to other forms of sex, which they did, or develop psycho-neurotic symptoms, which they did.

So they did defy the taboos, and foremost among the defiant were the clergy. Not only promiscuity but homosexuality and incest became prevalent among the clergy, as did those abuses that were available as a result of the control they had over people. A woman, for instance, could be denied absolution unless she offered herself to a priest.

There was at this time a widespread fear of impotence, which found its outlet when the witch-hunting began. A woman could be accused of having caused a man's impotence and suffer the loss of her life as a result of the accusation. (How could she possibly prove it was not true?)

We find in the histories of this period references to sodomy, flagellation, and sexual fantasies of a kind never before encountered. There was extensive fantasizing about the idea of a really satisfactory sexual encounter. There was the emergence of the imaginary incubi and succubi, beings who visited one at night for the purpose of sexual intercourse.

The Christian mystics of the time, if they were not obsessed with degrading themselves, were obsessed with the idea of being possessed by their Savior. Both in the writings and in the behavior of these people there is a great deal of eroticism. The way many of them described their relationship with Christ, and the feelings they had about him, would have exactly described a passionate physical union with a real person. Various symptoms experienced or described by nuns and other devotees and thought of as "divine possession" were very similar to those we would experience during intercourse and orgasm.

Self-abuse was very popular among the religious orders. There were individuals who inflicted wounds on themselves, who ate only garbage (or worse), who would wear only hair shirts, or who flagellated themselves regularly. Many of these people were canonized by the Church. The same acts, if performed today, would ensure the institutionalization of the participant.

One form of self-abuse that gained general acceptance was flagellation. At first discouraged by the Church, by the eleventh century it was extolled as a penance. By the middle of the thirteenth century there were large groups of people who met for this purpose. With the onslaught of the plague in the fourteenth century the incidence of self-flagellation increased and actually became a full-fledged movement.

As we can see, the Middle Ages were far from being the period of orderliness and morality that they are sometimes represented as being. They represent rather a cross between a charnel house and an insane asylum in which sadism and perversion, cruelty and abuse exploded on a scale which has seldom, if ever, been equaled. In comparison, the spontaneous lust of the Celtic predecessors is relatively subdued.

The picture we have now assembled of the Middle

Ages is very different from that of our childhood
storybooks. We have instead a picture of a time of
great depression, repression, and confusion. The new
Christian morality set man at odds with himself. He
was unavoidably sinful and he was subject to physical
and psychological abuse from all sides, whether he
was lay or clergy. Not only did really normal functions
become sins, and normal relationships become evil,
but normal feelings became forbidden.

Marriage, that relationship on which society seems
to depend so much for its stability, was incredibly
undermined by the Church's restrictions. If the aliena-
tion of the sexes did not begin in these times, it
nevertheless got a great boost. The Church supported,
even encouraged a woman in the name of her spirituality to deny her husband sexual favors. While this may
have been a fair weapon against male insensitivity and
the notion that sex was a man's right and a woman's
duty, it nevertheless led to incredible anger and frustration between married people.

Also, the impact of war and disease was a great
cause of social disorganization and demoralization.
The Christian knights in the Crusades, for example,
were not the pillars of virtue we have been led to
believe they were. All sorts of atrocities were committed by them in the name of Christ.

The plague in the fourteenth century was devastating in many ways and greatly undermined the power of
the Church, without changing any of the restrictions.
There was a period of frantic debauchery following the
plague. People didn't understand why they were being
punished. The plague would spare one and take another with no apparent motive. People participated in
all manner of sexual acts in an attempt to find the
magic that would save them from the ravages of disease, or else they were in despair that there was
nothing they could do about it.

Flagellation grew to enormous proportions. Bands
of flagellants roamed from town to town and grew to

such numbers that the Church took notice. The flagellants developed the belief that they could achieve salvation without the go-between of the Church, that through flagellation they could sufficiently purify themselves to save themselves from the plague and/or damnation. Of course, at this point the Church stepped in, and the movement was destroyed. Flagellation was then incorporated into the Church.

### The Inquisition: Sadism, Insanity, Torture, and Terror—All in the Name of the Lord

A little later on, the Inquisition became an instrument of repression in which all those who had any anger, frustration, or sadism could play a role in damaging and murdering, for the most part, innocent people. Originally the Church preached against the belief in witchcraft, but like so many other things, at some point it became conveniently incorporated into Church doctrine. In the fourteenth and fifteenth centuries witch-hunting became very popular, with the encouragement of the Church authorities.

In general, the trials of the Inquisition covered the following:

1) magic
2) heresy
3) worship of the devil
4) inexplicable illnesses
5) sexual delusions

At the beginning of the Inquisition there was an emphasis on the black magic of witches, but by the end of the fifteenth century the stress was almost entirely sexual. The ostensible battle against heresy was actually the continuation of the battle against sex.

The earliest activities of the Inquisition can be found in the thirteenth century, when the Church authorized the use of torture and attempted to wipe out the so-called Catharist heresy.

The Cathars were a group of people who attempted
to set up a model of reality that in many ways represented an attempt to return to the values and beliefs of
the early Christian communities. The Cathars believed
in sexual abstinence, and practiced it even when married, but they did not regard sex as sinful. They
believed that the spirit was enmeshed in matter, and
that avoidance of sex would speed up the process of
enlightenment. They evidently lived with one another,
men and women together, but chastely.

They were very interested in healing and in medi-
cine. (The Church at this time was violently against
scientific inquiry as well as any healing that appeared
to be magical.) The Cathars were nonviolent but did
undertake their own defense when attacked. They
believed in brotherly love reminiscent of the *agape* of
the early Christians. They were the earliest victims of
the Inquisition.

The persecution of the Cathars was just the beginning. The Inquisitors were preoccupied with sex to an
extreme degree, as were many of the denouncers of
the innocent. As we discussed earlier, the result of the
widespread prohibition of sexual activity on the part of
the Church resulted in galloping neurosis and even
psychosis.

Perhaps because the Church had developed the
ideas so fully that sex had the power to contaminate,
and that people could cause others to have a particular
sexual problem, i.e., they could bewitch them, all
sorts of accusations that today we would consider
crazy were not only taken seriously but were made the
grounds for the execution of many innocent people.

The largest source of victims of the Inquisition were
young teenage girls. One book on witchcraft of the
time states that "all witchcraft comes from carnal lust,
which in women is insatiable."

Any disease that doctors were unable to cure was
seen as having been caused by witchcraft. Epilepsy
and madness were therefore often said to be the result
of witchcraft, and the people accused of having caused

those illnesses often paid with their lives. A woman could lose her life because someone accused her of causing his impotence. (The revenge of a male angered by the refusal of sexual favors on the part of the accused?)

## The Devil Made Them Do It

The Devil became important in religion for the first time. Originally he was thought of only as an angel who had erred, but he now became the avowed enemy of God and man. And just as the troubador's Cult of the Lady inspired the development of the Virgin Mary as an important Church figure, so did the Inquisition bring about the development of the Devil as evil personified. The dichotomies were complete. On one hand there were the Devil and witches, on the other hand the Virgin Mary and Christ. Anyone accused of being a witch or in any way in league with the Devil became the enemy of God and therefore the Church.

The sadism of the Inquisitors has been well documented. Tortures were designed to keep the victim alive until he or she admitted guilt. The admission of guilt did not mean that the victim was freed, however. It served only to validate the Inquisitors themselves, and the awful program they were carrying out, and it nearly always ensured that the victim would lose his life. The difference was usually that if one admitted guilt, one was not burned or hanged alive but killed first. In the case of burnings, this was undoubtedly a mercy.

The ecclesiastical courts needed the sanction of the civil courts to carry out their program, because the ecclesiastical courts could not sentence people to death. They could only recommend a person be sentenced to death and hand him over to the civil authorities. It's important to remember that in the Middle Ages the sexual and religious codes imposed by the Church were not part of the legal structure. Civil law was separate from ecclesiastical law. Sexual matters as well as questions of heresy were almost entirely the province of the ecclesiastical courts.

In time, many of the prohibitions initiated by the Church became civil law, but during the Inquisition this was not the case. Adultery, homosexuality, and suicide were not governed by civil law. In England the change occurred during the reign of Henry VIII when he proclaimed himself the spiritual and temporal leader of the country. The power of the ecclesiastical courts was then abolished and all their laws were absorbed into the civil legal system.

But to return to the time of the Inquisition. As examples of the kind of things that went on: In 1400 the civil courts consented to recognize copulation with the Devil as a capital crime; in 1450 the proposition that witches engaged in night flight became Church dogma.

Hundreds and hundreds of people were put to death for witchcraft over a two-hundred-year period. Wars, the plague, and the Inquisition produced a population decline in Europe during these years.

The Protestants, by the way, did their own share of witch-hunting both in Europe and in America. In Scotland the churches provided boxes for anonymous denunciations. Calvin burned heretics of all kinds.


## The Renaissance: Times Improve—Sort Of

The period that emerged at the end of the Inquisition is known to us as the Renaissance. We think of it as a period of great artistic and literary flowering, and so it was. The social mores also underwent something of a flowering. The status of women was enhanced. More education was available to them, and they enjoyed more freedom socially. The pervading sense of guilt diminished during this period, especially in relation to sex. Dress became more elaborate. These times saw the reemergence of the courtesan, reminiscent of the days of classical Greece. These women of charm, intelligence, education, and manners enjoyed friendships with men of influence and power and had a great deal of freedom socially.

Unfortunately, what also flowered during this period was a kind of conscienceless violence. It was not the sadism or the obsessive violence of the Inquisition, but the indifferent violence of men and women who had lost respect for all authority, both ecclesiastical and civil. The calculated seduction of helpless and often unwilling young girls was common. The Marquis de Sade and the philosophy that pain inflicted upon unwilling victims in the pursuit of one's own pleasure was justified were products of this time. This development apparently was one consequence of the absolute loss of respect for authority that resulted from a corrupt Church demanding obedience to repressive laws in the face of its own conscienceless abuse of power and its internal corruption.

Prostitution was common in this era. The fear of impotence was again evident. Flagellation reappeared for a return engagement, along with a rise in the incidence of homosexuality. There developed a general effeminacy among men, who took to the use of cosmetics and very rich dress. The relationship between men and women was basically one of enmity. Women, however, had a good deal of freedom, or at least the courtesans did. The only mode of existence open to women who wished to be self-supporting was marriage, unless they chose the life of a courtesan. The taboos on unmarried sex remained, but those regarding adultery were greatly relaxed.

It was out of this time that the system of honor that produced the duel arose. The excessive concern for one's honor and the necessity of defending oneself against the smallest slights were a manifestation of the lawlessness and lack of respect for authority that existed at the time.

## The Reformation: Trading Disorder
## for Suppression

It was out of that same outrage at the abuses of the Church that the Reformation emerged. The Reformation was that tremendous Protestant movement fueled by the centuries of the Church's abuse of power. In Europe, the Reformation followed the Renaissance; in England these two movements developed at the same time. In England the reformers were the minority party, and many of them ended up in Holland and America, thus endowing New England with the stern and puritan morality for which it has become renowned.

The despair and confusion as a result of the plague, the growing lawlessness and disrespect for authority, and the inability of the Church to correct its excesses all contributed to the emergence of a new religious movement which in many ways was as suppressive as the order it sought to displace.

Neither alternative was any more supportive of people's happiness and well-being. Luther and Calvin in leading the revolution against the Church of Rome maintained that the Earth was the dominion of the Devil and that all forms of earthly pleasure were his weapons of seduction.

In England the concurrence of the Renaissance and Reformation resulted in a heightened consciousness of individual freedom without the lawlessness of Italy. The English became more frank about sex during this time. In England, Henry VIII united—for the first time in hundreds of years—spiritual and temporal power in one person. Criminal jurisdiction was removed from the ecclesiastical courts as they were stripped of their power. The result was that what had before been only a spiritual crime became a civil crime, punishable by imprisonment rather than penances or fines.

After a brief spring of some sexual freedom, the Reformation in England and the Continent brought a return to a winter of older sexual attitudes, with a vengeance and some new twists.

## Calvinism: Guilt-edged Religion and Pleasure as a Sin

The form of Protestantism that most influenced England was that of John Calvin. The religion as manifested in society supported the belief in witchcraft, the inferiority of women, and the divine authority of the Bible as the literal word of God. (The principle of the infallibility of the Bible was substituted for the infallibility of the Pope.) Calvin stressed paternal authority. In Geneva, for example, a child was beheaded for striking his father.

John Calvin could not be described as a fun guy. People who criticized his sermons were punished with three days of bread and water. A man who criticized Calvin himself was beheaded for treason and blasphemy. Calvin was fanatically against intellectual freedom. He constructed the strictest theocratic society ever devised. He treated with savage severity all those who disagreed with him. To impose his standards he resorted to violence, torture, and execution. All this in the name of God! On the other hand, the virtue of virginity was abandoned, polygamy was not considered evil and was sometimes legalized when war severely reduced the population.

A major feature of Calvinism was the generalization of feelings of guilt to cover every conceivable form of pleasure. We've also seen this in the teachings of the Roman Catholic Church in the Middle Ages.

The Puritan believed that there was danger in any activity in which there was any kind of spontaneous expression on the part of anyone. A pervading fear of pleasure therefore was the basis for the Protestant reformers, just as it was for the Catholics of the Middle Ages. In seventeenth-century England there were numerous ordinances forbidding dancing and even walking and "loitering." Attendance at sermons was mandatory. Color, decoration, richness of dress or interior decoration were suppressed. Unlawful sex became for the first time a criminal offense rather than simply an infraction of religious law (we are still living out the results of this development) and there was great hostility towards art and learning.

Another feature of the Puritan who emerged from the Reformation was the obsessive fear of dirt. The Puritans associated "evil smells" with the Devil, and there was thought to be some association between man's excretory functions and the Devil. It is fascinating to note that Luther received his great moment of "enlightenment" when he was sitting on the privy. (A Freudian, by the way, would almost certainly diagnose Luther as being anally fixated.)

The emerging middle class found enough in the values of the Reformation to support it. Also from this class of people the idea of democracy was developed more fully than it had been since the days of the Greeks and Romans. The people of this class were prosperous merchants and artisans and members of guilds, who, through the institutions they created and through the society that grew up as a result, established the idea of authority instituted by the governed for their own convenience.

And so we have the emergence of middle-class morality, against which the Counter-Reformation of the Catholic Church made little headway. (The Counter-Reformation was characterized by an increasing authoritarianism which was against scientific research and freedom of thought. There were certain outlets provided for spontaneity, however.)

Middle-class morality placed great importance on honesty, public order, respect for property, and work. It was less concerned with bravery, prayer, and self-punishment. The doctrine of Calvinism, which made work a virtue, emphasized the hoarding of gains rather than their ostentatious expenditure (heaven forbid you should find pleasure in wealth!) and which even permitted usury up to a point, was much better calculated to appeal to the small entrepreneur than the rigidities of Catholicism. It is therefore no accident that it was the countries that embraced Protestantism that subsequently made the social, economic, and political advances to capitalism.

### The Victorian Age: Sex Goes from Sinful to Disgusting

The Victorianism of the nineteenth century did nothing to ease the repressive attitudes carried forward from the Reformation. Reform societies were established which were devoted to the improvement of Sunday observances, the abolition of prostitution, and the reduction of blasphemy. With the advent of the Evangelicalists, as they were called, fundamentalism became even more popular. The Bible was treated as the literal word of God. Original sin became much discussed. For instance, the pains of childbirth were thought to be God's punishment for Eve's sin, and bitter battles were fought—by men—against the use of chloroform to relieve the pains of childbirth. When it was first used in England in 1847, the Church protested that it was in defiance of religion.

Needless to say, the status of women during this time was not terrific. The difference, if any, between the attitudes of the medievalists and the Victorians is that the medievalists believed woman was the source of all sexual evil and the Victorians said she was sexless and incapable of having sexual responses. (What they meant was that a *virtuous* woman was incapable of sexual response.) Sex was not so much sinful as it was disgusting.

Thus we see the development of prudery. (A prude is one who *pretends* an ignorance he or she does not possess.) The Victorians, or rather the Calvinists and then the Fundamentalists, forbade the representation of *anything* that in any way related to sex or had any sexual connotations either pictorially or verbally. The Church in the Middle Ages preached against sex, but they had no objection to calling a thing by its name, whether it had to do with sex, the body, or excretory functions.

The Victorians not only didn't like such names—the words of the sexual vocabulary—but they became obsessed with any reference that might call to mind anything even vaguely sexual. Words like whore and fornication were forbidden, of course, but so also were words relating to childbirth and pregnancy, as well as words referring to body functions, including words like sweat, and any words that referred to the excretory functions. The laws against obscenity were used to suppress any discussion of birth control.

The Victorians were thus obsessed with sex. The Victorian underground produced a pornography of unprecedented richness. Their prostitutes could be jailed but not their pimps. Brothels were a big business. On prostitutes men vented all their negative feelings about women. (One is reminded of Jack the Ripper, who victimized only prostitutes.) Masturbation was a great concern of the Victorians, and they provided a source of horror stories about its terrible consequences.

Here we have a brief history of our sexual and, to some extent, our religious past. This past provided the impoverished model of sexual and emotional reality that Sigmund Freud attempted to unravel, beginning in the latter part of the nineteenth century. Given these circumstances, we can hardly consider it surprising that Freud concluded that the human species is fundamentally incestuous, animalistic, environmentally destructive and that "the goal of all life is death."

Freud believed that man was in constant conflict with himself and society. The virtuous person was one who repressed his impulses, while a sinful person enjoyed them. Freud went on to say that "hatred is at the bottom of all the relations of affection and love between human beings; hatred in relation to objects is older than love."

Freud, a truly remarkable man, unfortunately did us all a disservice in further promoting the existing idea that the suppression of our nature was essential to the evolution of a modern civilization. This did nothing to enrich our already impoverished model of what it means to be human!

This is in sharp contrast to the ideas advanced by Wilhelm Reich, who had, for a period, an association with Freud. Reich maintained that we must live naturally, i.e., in accordance with our nature. Reich believed that a fully functioning, spontaneous, and unsuppressed sexuality was inseparable from any valid definition of mental health.

Where does all this leave us, and what are the lessons contained in all this? At this point you may feel you are part of a television game show where the question now is "Will the real sexual reality please step forward?" As comforting as the thought may be that this could happen, it won't. All recorded attempts to legislate human goodness and morality have been a failure. It is well known to military commanders that the suppression of a soldier's sexuality enhances the ferocity with which he fights.

Our past has been one trip laid on top of another, and the whole lot has been laid on us in some way, shape, or form. Each of us is responsible for our own escape from this impoverished model of human sexuality, indeed, from the impoverished model of what it means to be human. The escape route is not always easy. As Margaret Mead succinctly pointed out, we cannot heal a sexually suppressed society by taking its clothes off.

## What Do We Really Want from Sex?

We want excitement and passion, of course, but I think that beyond that most of us are really looking to be received, really looking to experience being close, and being safe. We are looking for a friendship that is laced with a sense of humor and punctuated with good sex.

The passionate experiences of sexual love are the condiments of a great relationship; they are not the meal. The passion of human sexuality is the pepper, the salt, the ketchup, the mayonnaise, and the mustard, but it is surely not the entree! The existence of real friendship in the relationship is the meal.

We often see people piling a lot of pepper, salt, ketchup, mayonnaise, mustard, sometimes Worcestershire sauce and, if they are hip, tamari on their plate of relationships. It is certainly spicy, but hardly nourishing. And very shortly thereafter, they are hungry again.

What does life look like when sex is a pleasure and not an issue?

I notice a magical quality in the way people relate when they have resolved the issue of their own sexuality. They have come to peace with the concept and with the physical reality of their own sexuality and have arrived at the point where there is no compulsion about it anymore. Sex is now simply a choice. The way they relate to others is now different because there are no sexual undercurrents in their conversation unless they deliberately put them there.

## Is Happiness Possible?

It is probably more difficult today to have an intimate relationship that endures than it has been in the past. We have come to expect so much more from our relationships. I'm not saying that it is a mistake, but the idea of being happy and feeling satisfied and being joyful in relationships and in life is a radical idea of the middle part of the twentieth century. It wasn't until the fifties and sixties that we really began to pursue as a culture the possibility of being happy and fulfilled on a continuing basis.

For some people, the idea of happiness is still out of the question. One day I was talking to a woman who was, perhaps, in her mid-thirties. She had no idea who I was or what I did. She said to me, "Don't you think it's ridiculous that people talk about being happy? Everybody knows you're not supposed to be happy in this life. All you can hope for is to survive with the least amount of discomfort." There are still many people who don't think that the pursuit of happiness is important or even moral. They believe that the pleasure of personal fulfillment is not possible or desirable. I know that it is not only possible but also vital, because if we don't find our way to this place of inner reconciliation there will always be conflict, and we can no longer afford the price of conflict, because our ability to kill each other has become so sophisticated these days that the consequence of human conflict can now be very final.

In short, if we don't learn how to really make love instead of war, we will all perish.

# 10

## On Marriage

"What's this?" you ask. "Here we are, we've talked about sex, and now we're about to speak of marriage and we haven't even talked about love!" Yes, indeed.

Though we may seem to have the cart before the horse, the truth is that the notion that love and marriage go together like a horse and carriage is a tragic illusion, as we shall presently see.

## Why Does a Marriage Made in Heaven Turn Out to Be Hell?

For many of us, marriage—and family—represents the grand failure of the human species. Two people come together with the best of intentions and vow that they will love and support each other from this day forward. It seems simple enough.

But most marriages end up a far cry from where they began. What happens in the middle? What causes the breakdown that makes a lie out of our highest stated ideals? What is it that makes a mockery of the marriage vows and the stated intentions of lovers?

Why is it that marriages made in heaven seem to end up in hell? Our failure in marriage seems to be another demonstration of our powerlessness, of our inability to say what we want and make it happen. If power is the ability to act, to make something happen, to realize an intention, then we are not powerful at all, and our failure of not being able to live in close proximity with one another, the failure of marriage, seems to be irrefutable evidence that this is so.

But wait a minute. As we have seen in the previous chapter, our sexual mythology is an insane conglomeration of fears, guilt, expectations and attitudes, hormones and urges that has somehow become our model for achieving happiness in bed. Could it be that our models for marriage and relationships are just as much an unworkable product of our insane past as are our sexual models? If this is true, we have been tryng to win an impossible game. When we keep struggling to accomplish what we don't know is impossible, the consequences to our self-esteem are devastating.

Again, as we seek freedom for happiness, we begin by tracing the synthesis of our unworkable models from the customs and mythologies of the past.

### Alternate Models of Marriage: Ancient Athens and Sparta, Where Marriage Was Nothing Personal—Just Business

Marriage in ancient Greece was, as seems to have been the case during most of our history since that time, an institution created and regulated by the state or church for the support of the political or religious establishments.

In Homeric Greece, marriage was arranged by the parents and was essentially a purchase of the woman from her father. Love was not expected. If it was present, it came after marriage and was the product of a long domestic association between the couple.

In the very strict society established in Sparta, marriage was very closely regulated by the state. Of primary importance was the breeding of eugenically superior children. Public nudity on the part of both young men and young women was encouraged, so that defects could be seen and corrected. Young people were allowed cosiderable sexual freedom before marriage. The ideal age of marriage for men was thirty; for women, twenty. The marriages were usually arranged, although they were without the element of purchase that existed in Homeric times. Love again was something that developed after marriage rather than before.

In Sparta celibacy was a crime. Bachelors were disenfranchised by the state. There evidently was very little adultery* and divorce is said to have been rare.

---

*Note that the use of the term adultery reveals a double standard that persists to this day. If a married woman had a sexual liaison with any other man she was considered an adulteress. If a married man had a sexual liaison with another woman this was not considered adulterous unless she also happened to be married. In later times and in other cultures, when the act of adultery carried the death penalty, women only were executed, except in unusual circumstances when a man's transgression involved a married woman of the ruling order, in which case he may have been executed for treason.

POWER                                    163

In order to bring forth superior human specimens,
however, it was acceptable for older men to "loan"
their wives for reproductive purposes to relatives or
associates who were considered qualified paternity
candidates. This was also done if the husband was
impotent or sterile.

The Athenians departed from the Spartans in their
views on marriage not so much in essence as in degree.
Marriages were arranged in this society also, but there
were evidently more instances when the choice was
made by the couples themselves. Romantic love was
not a requirement or justification here either, as the
purpose of the marriage was to provide an orderly
means for the maintenance of property and also for the
propagation of children.

In Athens the women retained control of any property that was part of their dowry, and in the case of
divorce this was also retained by them. In the event of
divorce the children went to the father, however.

The Athenians also had laws against bachelorhood
for men, but they were not enforced as stringently as
they were in Sparta. Wives were also "loaned" to
brothers or other relatives when the husbands for
some reason were unable to beget children, and all
children who resulted from such unions were considered the legal issue of the husband. In all Greek
societies, as in other eras, men were allowed and
expected to seek sexual satisfaction outside of marriage. In times when the male population was greatly
reduced by war it was acceptable for a man to marry
two women.

In a number of schools of Eastern wisdom thought
to have influenced the teachings of Christ, marriages
were also to be arranged. Again this was done to
ensure orderly property transferral and the propagation of the species. Beyond that, these schools of
wisdom presented a further purpose for marriage,
namely, that it was a structure in which the partners
were to learn the lessons required for them to experience love towards another person (i.e., each other).

So, in a sense, marriage was seen as a school for love. This is an eminently workable model, as long as we remain clear that we are not talking about romantic love. We will return to this concept later on.

From various philosophers through the ages, we discover that romantic love in marriage was not considered an issue, nor was it even considered particularly desirable. Some thought it was not even possible. Especially in Sparta, but also in Athens, the society was so structured that very little opportunity existed for men and women to spend much time together, suppressing the possibility of romantic involvement.

In Sparta, for instance, boys were taken from their homes at the age of seven and spent the next twenty-three years in dormitories exclusively in the company of others of their own sex. Even if they married before the age of thirty, their place of residence remained the barracks. They visited their wives only briefly and primarily for the purpose of begetting a family.

Except for a very small class of women, Greek women did not receive the same kind of education as did the men, so husbands and wives were left without much chance of developing a relationship on an intellectual basis. Additionally, there seem to have been few restrictions on relationships between men, and whether or not they were of a sexual nature, they were primarily what was available and were acclaimed as being the most desirable. Some Greeks regarded the highest form of love as that between two men. This may or may not have been expressed physically.

One of the most noble relationships was considered to be that between an older man and a youth. The youth was for the man the object of special attention and devotion, and he in turn looked to the older man as his teacher and mentor. A boy who was not chosen by an older man for this kind of relationship was something of a disgrace. The relationship was considered as important as the parental relationship.

Within marriage, many men and women undoubtedly came to have a great deal of affection for each other, perhaps even passion, but it is important for us to recognize that marriage was not seen as an expression of this devotion or passion, or even as a context in which to explore these feelings. Marriage was designed to ensure the continuation of the species; more, it was designed to ensure the birth of the strongest and healthiest and most intelligent children possible. It was also a means for men to acquire or add to their assets, in the form of the dowry or marriage portion received from the bride's family.

It should also be emphasized that there were very few, if any, social or legal restrictions on physical relations between or among the sexes. Homosexuality, while it may have been shunned by many, was certainly not a crime. It may have been a crime to be a bachelor after a certain age, but it was not a crime for a man to have a sexual relationship with another man, and apparently the same freedom was available to women, at least to that class of women who would be considered today as courtesans and mistresses.

The courtesans had the most freedom of any group of women in Greek society. They were the most educated and many were very wealthy. There was no stigma attached to what they did, and the most intelligent and charming of them were received in the highest circles. They were often the lovers of rulers and philosophers. They, more than any other women, had the opportunity to have satisfying relationships with men. If they became attached to one in particular they became much more than lovers, fulfilling the role of companion and advisor as well.

## Tenth-Century England: Trial Marriages and Swinging Scene, Then Business as Usual

If we jump from classical Greece to the England of the tenth century, we find a very different society, but one whose attitudes towards marriage were in many ways similar. The most significant of these is that, as far as we know, romantic love was not a requirement or an inducement for the union. Here again we find love to be insufficient grounds for a marriage.

We have only a little knowledge of the Celts and Saxons, but we do know that the Irish of this period were strongly matriarchal. Marriage was not indissoluble. Marriages were often entered into on a trial basis, and liaisons even more temporary were formed. Polygamy was not uncommon. Frequent changes of partners were usual until late in the Middle Ages.

In the Christianized versions of many of the folktales of this period, the conquering knight is often offered the king's daughter in marriage, but in the earlier versions, marriage is not part of the deal, while a one-night stand invariably was. Women were free to take lovers, both before and after marriage, and men were free to seduce all women of lower rank and to solicit the favors of women of equal or higher rank through some demonstration of valor. Marriage was often regarded as a temporary liaison.

## The Church Unveils Lifelong Monogamy with No Possibility of Parole

These were the circumstances awaiting the Catholic missionaries of the Middle Ages as they arrived in what is now known as Great Britain. The Church's first goal was to establish the principle of lifelong and monogamous marriage.

There were two reasons for the importance of this goal. Without it the strict sexual codes that followed would have been meaningless, and it also ensured the legal inheritance of property, which in a paternalistic society necessitates that a man know for certain that his son is indeed his son.

Marriage in the Middle Ages was still a private contract between individuals. Even witnesses were not required. If the couple adhered to the new faith, the blessing of the Church might be sought, but its absence did not invalidate the marriage. All that was needed was that the two people state their intention, and within the laws of consanguinity, the marriage was valid.

The Church distinguished between illegal and invalid marriages. A marriage without a priest was illegal, according to Church law, and might result in penance, but it was not invalid. Not until the 1600s was the presence of a priest necessary to make the marriage valid, and by that time England had repudiated the Roman Catholic Church.

One way the Church worked towards its ideal of the lifelong monogamous marriage was to make divorce almost impossible. In fact, legal divorce was impossible; the only avenues were annulment or separation. If the couple separated, they of course were not free to marry anyone else. An annulment could be obtained only by proving that one had married someone who was too close in kin, that one had unknowingly married one's sibling, or other close blood relative. This became a source of one of the greatest abuses in the Church, because annulments could be bought upon payment to the Church of various sums of money.

Incompatibility, impotence, barrenness as grounds for divorce were inadmissible. When you consider that people did not marry for love but for political or social reasons, and if one or the other partner could not fulfill his or her end of what was more openly than now a contract, it seems indeed unfair that the Church removed the possibility of either party nullifying that contract through divorce.

## Loving Your Mate Sexually Becomes a Sin

The other program initiated by the Church was to regulate the sexual behavior of everyone, married and unmarried, by means of a code that ensured that any pleasure people received from sex was purely accidental. The code stated that sex should be avoided if possible, even among married people. Of course, it was totally forbidden to unmarried people.

The encouragement of celibacy among married people led to the notion that it was spiritually good for wives to sexually deny their husbands. This at first might seem like the beginning of some kind of liberation for wives from the notion that it was their duty to be sexually available to their husbands on demand. But in fact, if this did not begin the deep-seated antagonism between the sexes, it ensured its continuance. On the one hand, the husbands, if they followed the Christian faith, had the right of property over their wives. Wives had no legal status and were in every way subject to the will of their husbands ("and the two shall be as one," as the Bible says, "only the man is the master"). On the other hand, according to the Church's sexual code, women were entirely within their spiritual rights to deny their husbands access to their bodies.

In a similar vein, the Church took the position that it was a sin not only to experience pleasure in sex, but also to experience desire for someone, even one's spouse. To support the suppression of someone's desire thus became a virtue, even if that person was your husband. In essence, the Church placed a ban on all forms of sex other than nonpleasurable intercourse between married people for the sole purpose of procreation.

Furthermore, it was directed that only the "missionary" position could be used; other positions were forbidden. There was a limit to the number of days on which sex could occur. It could not be performed on certain Church holidays, nor on Sundays, Wednesdays, or Fridays, forty days before Easter, forty days before Christmas, or from the time of conception until forty days after the birth of the child. Of course, there were laws against abortion.

As far as the Church was concerned, an engagement became a marriage if the parties engaged in sex, whether or not they actually married.

It is interesting to note that the attitudes of the very early Christian Church towards marriage were very different from those imposed by the Christian missionaries on the "heathen" people of Britain.

Marriage for the early Christians was considered a proper course of action for those who felt unable to sublimate their sexual desires. St. Paul said that sexual abstinence was desirable but considered it a gift from God that many never receive. He specifically said that it was not sinful to marry. His teachings have been twisted to justify the idea that sex and marriage are unholy. The very early Christian Church recognized divorce on such grounds as barrenness and religious incompatibility.

In Jewish law of classical times there was no ban on premarital sex. A married man might have a mistress, which was not considered adultery, and prostitution was allowed. A married woman did not have the same freedom, because it affected the right of property.

Monogamous marriage has become so much a part of our cultural model that we assume it has always everywhere been the custom. It has not. Even though endorsed for the last thousand years by the Catholic Church and by almost every Protestant religion, there were times when Europe was ravaged by wars and the male population so decimated that it was declared lawful for a man to have more than one wife. This did not occur often, but it does illustrate that even a code as stringent as that of the Church turned out to be flexible, if only temporarily, when the motive was strong enough.

The notion that marriage is the proper outcome of the personal preoccupation which we ambiguously call "love" is a modern one. In fact, it is an idea introduced to us, for the most part, by the English Romantic poets, and it has been taken seriously nowhere except in Great Britain, Australia, parts of Europe, and the United States. Most of us are raised to believe that marrying for love and living, if not happily ever after, at least satisfactorily ever after, is a reasonable expectation, and we further believe this has always been so. But, in fact, it is less than two hundred years ago that the Romantics introduced this radical, new model of marriage embodying the following ideas:

1) Marriage depends upon the mutual love of both parties.
2) Men and women have equal rights. (Some of the wives and lovers of these poets were the pioneers of today's women's liberation movement, women such as Mary Wollstonecraft, for example.)
3) Romantic love should be the *raison d'être* of the marriage relationship.
4) There is no distinction between *eros* and *agape* (physical desire and chaste affection). Sensual passion and platonic companionship should both be present in a marriage relationship.
5) Premarital sex is acceptable.
6) Each person has a twin soul somewhere in the world, and if one can only find that person, one could live happily ever after.

These ideas existed in complete contrast and conflict with all those previously held by the Church, by the society of early England, and by the culture of classical Greece, all of which maintained that marriage was not dependent upon love, and that any two people not obviously antipathetic could have an effective marriage.

There were certain consequences to this new way of thinking. First of all, this new romantic model implied nothing could be allowed to stand in the way of possessing the perfect person, once he or she was found. In other words, nothing could be allowed to stand in the way of true love. (More about this later.)

There were several famous instances of *ménages à trois*. These marked an attempt to bring to marriage both intellectual companionship and sexual passion. George Eliot (Mary Anne Evans) lived for a period of time in the household of a man she greatly esteemed. We don't really know what the nature of the relationship was, but her relationship with the man's wife was uncomfortable and resulted in her leaving the household. Wordsworth and Byron both found themselves in the unenviable position of being in love with their sisters.

Wordsworth went on to a happy marriage, but one wonders what such people go through if they attempt to carry their ideas to their logical conclusions. Whatever way they handled their own personal relationships, their legacy to us is clear: Romantic love within marriage had been launched as an ideal.


## The Troubadors: Falling in Love with Love

The troubadors of the twelfth century and the Romantics of the nineteenth century have much in common in their concept of romantic love. The great difference is that the troubador never saw marriage as the desired outcome of passionate love. In fact, the troubador believed that passionate love between married people was impossible. If the troubadors were the first to make a virtue of passionate love, the Romantics were the first to make a virtue of it in marriage.

In the United States today, the terms "love" and "marriage" are still almost synonymous. When we fall in love, we are apt to at least ask ourselves the question, "Am I going to marry this person?"

No other civilization we know of has embarked with anything like the same ingenuous assurance upon the perilous enterprise of making marriage coincide with passion and romantic love, and of making the first depend upon the second.

Where does this leave us? Hopefully with an awareness that we have distilled a collection of conflicting ideals, gathered from the past, into our dreams of a future that is at odds with reality. The codes of conduct that Church and state would impose upon our lives stand in opposition to our yearning for the passionate experience and our romantic dreams, and both of these models remain incompatible with any attainable reality of relationship and marriage that could nurture and enrich us as participants.

The hardest task at the outset is to ask ourselves to give up our dreams. We have journeyed to ancient Greece a number of times in this exposition, and here is yet another illumination for us. In the mythology of ancient Greece we find the story of Pandora.

According to legend, Pandora was made in heaven, every god contributing something to perfect her. Venus gave her beauty, Mercury persuasion, Apollo music, and so on. Thus equipped, she was conveyed to Earth as the first woman, where she became the partner of Epimetheus.

One lovely evening, while dancing together, they beheld the arrival of Mercury, Jupiter's messenger, staggering beneath the weight of a huge box which rested upon his shoulders. Pandora immediately ceased dancing to speculate with feminine curiosity upon the contents of the box. Mercury asked permission to deposit his burden in their dwelling for safekeeping and promised to return for it shortly.

It was not long before Pandora's desire to have a peek at the contents of the box had her deft fingers busily at work untying the knot of glittering cord that held fast the lid. The knot yielded and Pandora raised the lid to have just one little peek at the contents.

Unfortunately—for us all—Jupiter had malignantly crammed into this box all the diseases, sorrows, vices, crimes, and sufferings that afflict humanity to this very day, and the lid was no sooner raised a fraction, than all these afflictions flew out in the guise of horrid little brown-winged creatures, closely resembling moths. (At this point a comparison of Pandora and Eve becomes too obvious to ignore.)

Pandora, in surprise and pain, dropped the lid shut, only to hear a sweet voice from inside the box plead: "Open, open, and I will heal your wounds! Please let me out!"

It was well for Pandora that she opened that box a second time, for the gods had concealed among the evil creatures one kindly spirit, Hope, whose mission was to heal the wounds inflicted by her fellow prisoners.

Well, how does this illuminate the darkness of the pain in our relationships? The illumination is this: Hope is not all that she appears to be, for this kindly spirit can unwittingly become our jailer. We can find ourselves the prisoner of Hope, and nowhere is this confinement more prevalent than in our romantic relationships.

Hope implies that some source external to ourselves is going to save us from the darkness of our pain and endow us with a happy-ever-after. Guess what: This isn't going to happen.

It is Hope that harnesses us in relentless pursuit of the unattainable dream, which is not to say all dreams are unattainable, but to say that we would be wise to give up those that are.

Which dreams to give up? What constitutes the unattainable? Namely this: a dream that exists in an unworkable reality. These are the dreams we must be willing to give up to fully have the gift of our life. This should not be interpreted as a denunciation of the institution we call marriage or any model of a relationship that includes long-term sexual fidelity.

Clearly there are those of us for whom this works beautifully. Upon a close examination of those marriages that endure through time as a source of inspiration and comfort, we find that the partners regard their marriage as a context in which they have developed the awareness and skills necessary to experience respect, friendship, love, and support for another person, their spouse.

Moreover, such partners share with me that they feel they have had many relationships over the years; they have just been with the same person. In fact, upon further reflection, they usually go on to say, not only have they had many relationships over the years, they have had them with different people of the same name.

In other words, not only have they been adaptable to changing roles within the marriage, they have evolved to regard these changing roles, together with their own and their partner's personal changes, with an air of excitement. In the concluding chapter of this book we will examine in some depth a workable model of a relationship that allows for a quality of experience you may not even have dreamed of.

Meanwhile, let's talk about love.

# LOVE

# 11

## An Introduction to Love

If you really want an insight into the primary preoccupation of a particular culture, listen to the lyrics of its contemporary songs. In our culture, the lyrics reveal a primary fixation on something we call "love." For the most part, our songs are about the ecstasy of finding love or the agony of losing it. What is love, anyway?

Love has been a central theme of art, literature, music, and poetry throughout time. We could reasonably expect that a subject commanding so much attention and interest would by now have become experientially understood. Alas, however, such is not the case.

What is this magical element, this transfiguring force, which we liken to "a trip to the moon on gossamer wings," and without which "life just ain't worth living"? What is this thing called love?

### What Is Love?

Before we attempt an answer to this question, we should first stop and recognize how rare it is that we should even have the opportunity to ask it. Because very few cultures have ever achieved the level of material well-being to allow the apparent luxury of contemplating such a question.

The culture of ancient Greece, a civilization that evolved to a high level of philosophical excellence, directed a good deal of attention to probing the mysteries of love. They differentiated between various kinds of love, and in shedding some light on the riddle of what is love, so shall we.

Specifically, we will be talking about three kinds of love: instinctual love, romantic love, and conscious love.

As we explore answers to the question "What is love?" we will make the discovery that to ask it is no mere luxury but is essential to our personal and planetary survival.

# 12

## Instinctual Love

When we are experiencing the "warm fuzzies," we are experiencing instinctual love. This is the love that we feel for each other when no fear stands between us. Quite simply, then, the experience of this kind of love requires our letting go of fear.

We do not "fall" into instinctual love. Instinctual love just *is;* it simply exists, waiting to be discovered so that it may warm and heal our lives. This is the love that endures through the ages to hold, to heal, and to maintain what continues to exist as the human family. This love cares in a profoundly personal way. It is a vital ingredient in all relationships, be they friendships, marriages, romances, or business partnerships.

Instinctual love protects life when it is vulnerable. It can be seen in the interaction between a mother and her child, between a lioness and her cubs, between a doe and her fawn. It lives within each of us, as a powerful desire to nourish, to protect, to foster growth, to teach. We feel this love stir within us when we hold a baby in our arms, or we shed our tears as we watch the movie *Bambi*.

Instinctual love is the essence of life itself.

Nothing can flourish where it is absent. While this kind of love is the most intimate, private experience we can have, it is also the most universal. When Christ said, "Love one another," this is the love to which he referred.

Plato did his best to point civilization in the right direction when he told us that "the essence of man is to seek a suitable recipient for his love."

It is a strange and tragic thing that this love which is our natural state has become so rarely part of our daily experience. Why? The answer is fear. When fear leaves, love fills its place. The next question is, of course: How can we be free of fear? In earlier chapters we talked about ways of managing our reactions in life as a path to emotional freedom, all of which applies in answer to this question. We should now advance this discussion a little further.

There is a specific goal that we can set for ourselves in life, the pursuit of which will free us from fear and fill our lives with love, and the goal is peace of mind. Peace of mind becomes ours as we exchange our unworkable models of reality for models that do work. We must come to recognize that the standards and judgments and restrictions that have been imposed on us by others and that have been a source of so much pain were imposed on us in ignorance. It is time to view the past in the spirit of forgiveness.

The key to our peace of mind is forgiveness. This begins with our forgiveness of ourselves and must be in the next instant followed by our forgiveness of others. The terrible things that we appear to do to each other are a product of our fears, so we must first forgive ourselves and others for all our reactions to fear. To be afraid is a natural phenomenon, but we do not have to react. We can train ourselves not to react but to respond creatively instead. As we stop reacting, others around us will cease to react. The effects are miraculous.

In a world filled with pain and negativity, we have become conditioned to focus on the ways in which we feel others have caused us pain and loss. Similarly, others focus their attention on the ways they believe we have caused them pain and loss. All of which makes for a climate of fear. The solution is to shift focus. Just as a photographer can select a sharp focus in his photographic representation of the world, so can we select to focus on the positive aspects of our world, rather than those aspects we hold to be negative.

I have witnessed people in the process of destroying their relationship and themselves by attaching more importance to the 20 percent that wasn't working than to the 80 percent that was wonderful. Avoid the same mistake. Instead, develop selective memory, whereby you retain most clearly in your mind the beautiful and nurturing elements of others and of your life. Do this moment by moment in your daily experience by training yourself to look for what is good and beautiful rather than for something to criticize.

An atmosphere of criticism is an atmosphere of fear, and is therefore without love. By developing our selective memory and selectively forgetting the moments of pain and loss in our past, we will no longer be afraid that the present is going to turn out like the past.

### The Past Does Not Cause the Present or Dictate the Future

This is a very important idea. The past may appear to cause the present but only because we use it to create our climate of fear, to which we then react, thereby reinforcing the reality of our fear. This we have seen as a principle earlier in this book.

When we are no longer under the fear of criticism, we come alive. The fear of criticism, or the fear of disapproval, keeps our creativity prisoner. As we cease criticizing others out of our own fear, our own fear of criticism will begin to disappear, to be replaced by peace of mind and the stirrings of love.

Complete and open communication displaces fear and creates the room for our experience of instinctual love. Complete and open communication takes courage, because in the process we must tell each other all the things that we are afraid to tell each other, all the while experiencing our experience rather than reacting to it. This is no easy task. However, if we will find within ourselves the courage and compassion to be open and complete in our communication with each other, we will come into the experience of "I love you."

Remember, love is the truth, all else is a lie.

# 13

## On Romantic Love

Romantic love has been the subject of deification and worship throughout the rise and fall of all civilizations. The idealized eroticism of love that pervades our contemporary culture was described by Plato as "a certain kind of madness."

Traditionally, romantic or passionate love has been feared by the mighty and the powerful for its disruptive effects on an otherwise well-reasoned life. To the Greeks, Eros, the god of love, was the personification of timeless desire—the original heavy breather. From the very beginning Eros was idolized, worshipped, and served. He was also considered a force to be feared for the havoc he could cause. After all, Eros represented the irresistible attraction between two people that could deprive them of all sense of proportion and, if taken to its ultimate end, could destroy them both.

During this period of antiquity, love was embodied in a mythology and has remained enshrouded in that mythology ever since. But whether it's a romantic legend from the Middle Ages or the lyrical lament of a country and western ballad, the power that this myth wields over our lives and the way we live them is much mightier than we realize.

The very quality of human life—your life, my life— is determined by the models of reality that we inherit and embellish as we live. We attempt to make yesterday's illusion today's reality. All the lies and standards, all the shoulds and ought-to's, all the fears and attitudes, all the legends and cultural archetypes—all the elements of a "way to be"—are collected and combined into a mythology of powerlessness and fear that we use to define ourselves as individuals and as a species. As unworkable illusions merge with whatever we ordinarily call reality, we become insane.

The most profound characteristic of a mythology is the power that it wins over us, usually without our knowledge. The very statement of a myth disarms all criticism (after all, it's only a myth), and reason, if not silenced, becomes at best ineffective.

We accept and agree to this model for living and then create experiences to fit within it, thereby reinforcing the power that the mythology holds over us.

In this chapter we will examine the origins of our unworkable model of romantic love—a model that has ensured the enduring sadness and dissatisfaction of our race, that has made life an endless game of gain and loss that keeps us as eternal seekers, prolonging forever the day when we stop and find, within ourselves, our own power for happiness.

Today the mythology of romantic love provides the images that fill the background of our lives. Our mechanical boredom intensifies our desire for "escape" and, as a result, everything within us and about us glorifies passion. The prospect of a passionate experience has come to mean that we are about to live more fully and more intensely. Many of us regard life as just the mundane filler between romances. In fact, the human epic we call our history could be viewed as a seemingly endless series of love stories with sad endings and tragic consequences.

We look upon passion as a transfiguring force— something beyond delight and pain, a state of blessedness. And yet, for most of us, passionate love is a misfortune. In this respect, matters have undergone no change for centuries. Indeed, the word "passion" means, literally, a suffering, although today the word more broadly means an enthusiasm or fondness or strong love or affection.

It is also important to note at this point, since we are speaking of romantic love, that the word "romantic" is defined by Webster as "having no basis in fact; fanciful." This is a major clue in finding the source of our suffering.

It is no wonder that romantic love and confusion travel hand in hand, for the components of the mythology are complex and often contradictory.

To find where we gathered our ideas of romantic love, we must explore the status that romance and passion have been given in different societies throughout history.

### The Early Greeks: Masters of Love

The Greeks distinguished from among several different kinds of love, just as we do, and many of these correspond. The Greeks distinguished between devotion, tenderness, physical desire, gratitude, generosity, friendship, ecstasy, and disinterested love. Their language included the necessary specialized vocabulary to allow subtle differentiations of love to be communicated.

Their word *agape* signified the loving concern for everyone. The yearly festival of the Agape was held to celebrate and foster nonsexual, nonhierarchical love among all people, and it became part of early Christian tradition.

The Greek word *philia* translates most closely as friendship, but the Greeks used *philia* to describe four different types of friendship: the first, the affection felt for blood relations; the second, the friendship of a host for his guests; the third, the concept of friendship as we generally think of it; and the fourth, passionate friendship or the profound ties that may exist between persons either of the same or of different sexes.

*Mania* represented frenzied passion or ecstasy. According to Socrates there were four kinds of ecstasy; prophetic, religious, poetic, and, most elevated of all, amorous ecstasy. The last was considered the most precious of all. A mania was tantamount to a divine passion, and a person so affected was considered to be possessed by the gods, and therefore blessed, and consequently not subject to mortal laws. This last idea becomes central to the developing mythology and survives to this day.

Eros, the god of love, was said to have been born at the same time as the world itself and was called "the desired one." He caused the sky and earth to unite. He was the creative urge, the god of the lover and his beloved, the personification of an elementary force of nature. He was love invincible, and, according to the mythology, no one could escape his grasp.

Moreover, the Greeks believed that knowing the mysteries of love would ensure immortality, and that these mysteries were revealed by the gods to those who knew in their hearts that their love was stronger than death. The Greeks saw, in passionate love, the imminence of a higher reality. They were not talking exclusively about sex, but about the ecstasy of love to which sex can be a means. Amorous ecstasy denoted the quality of the emotion felt by the two people and not the actuality of a sexual union.

In the folklore of ancient India, we find the notion that there are five degrees of love. The first is that of servant for master (or mortal for God); the second, of friend for friend; the third is that of parent for child; the fourth is that of spouses for each other. The fifth is passionate or illicit love. This last notion enters and remains as a significant theme of our own mythology

So the notion of passion or ecstasy or romantic love was familiar to other cultures existing long before our time and was accorded a very special place in those cultures—perhaps even more of a special place than we accord it today. Apparently, there was very little guilt associated with passion, as described by the commentators of past eras. Passion was an acknowledged part of the spectrum of love.


## The Origins of Our Own Mythology

Let's bring our exploration of romantic love a little closer to our time—to that period from the past which we today think of as the embodiment of all of our fondest fantasies regarding romantic love. The eleventh, twelfth, and thirteenth centuries left us the stories of knights in shining armor killing dragons and saving princesses, stories of witches and beautiful maidens and chivalrous men and high honor and virtue and true love and happy endings.

Or so we imagine. Little of this is true. The stories and legends of that time are highly romantic, i.e., they have little basis in fact. They are filled with adventure and love, and in the most influential of them we find tragic endings (as we think of tragic). And all of the stories, whether happy or tragic, whether told to us as children or absorbed through osmosis as we live in our culture, affect the way we think about romantic love.

The mythology itself is confused. We think of handsome knights in shining armor if we are women, and beautiful and virtuous maidens if we are men, and we yearn for a world where such creatures exist. We have forgotten or do not seem to know that the knights in shining armor, the beautiful maidens, and a world where grand and glorious passion is possible are only part of a fanciful story.

## Enter the Troubadors: Passion Becomes a Career

In the beginning of the twelfth century in France a movement headed by poets, or "troubadors," as they were called, came into existence. It has been called the "Cult of the Lady" by some historians.

Ostensibly, this was what happened: Each troubador chose as the object of his devotion a particular lady, usually the lady of his patron or lord, but apparently always a woman of high birth who in most cases was married. He referred to her as his mistress, and the word as we know it today derives from the relationship thus created by the troubadors, and which means now, as it meant then, an enduring nonmarital relationship between a man and a woman.

The difference between a mistress today and one then is that the relationship between a troubador and his mistress was apparently nonsexual, or at least it was not consummated. Physical contact was in many cases apparently permitted, even desired, but the purpose of such contact was to inflame passion, not to satisfy it. In fact, the relationship was established and conducted for the purpose of thwarting desire—for inflaming desire and not satisfying it.

For troubadors, the kind of experience they wanted was the product of the frustration of desire. They

wanted neither marriage nor consummation sexually
with their ladies or mistresses. They believed that the
desire they felt would vanish if it were satisfied. They
never saw marriage as a desired outcome of passionate
love.

While they believed deep affection was possible,
and while there is every indication that they had
sexual relationships with people other than their mistresses, the actuality of friendship and sexual union
was absent from their relationship with the object of
their passion.

There is a theory that this movement—the Cult of
the Lady—was actually religious, and that the adulation of a particular lady and the poems and songs that
were written in praise of her were actually the worship
of Mary, the mother of Jesus, in disguise. The fertility
cults that were supplanted by the Christian religion
worshipped a female figure, or several of them, and in
the societies overrun by Catholic missionaries women
played an important part.

Whether the movement *was* an old religion coming
out in the weave of the new Catholic one, whether it
was a new religion which felt it had to remain secret,
or whether it was not religious at all, the movement
had several consequences.

One was that the Church attacked it vigorously.
Another is that the "Cult of the Lady" contributed to
the development within the Church of the "Cult of the
Virgin Mary." She became important as a go-between
for sinners to plead their case before God, whereas she
had not been important before. The Virgin Birth,
which was not a doctrine of the Early Church, now
became official dogma. Here we have an example of
the Church's tendency to stamp out heresy (i.e., the
Cult of the Lady) and then include it in its own dogma
at a later date (in this case, as the Cult of the Virgin).

The model of passionate romantic love created by
troubadors was based on the contemplation of the
beauty of the beloved, and the creation of a union of

hearts and minds—rather than bodies—of the lovers. This love was thought to be the source of all goodness and virtue and to inspire goodness and virtue in the lover by contemplation of the loved one. It is a passionate love, not to be confused with the chaste *agape* or disinterested love practiced by the early Christians. As such, the model pursues and encourages all that fans and provokes desire, short of actual intercourse.

The value of this idea was that a man would not do anything that would disgrace him in the eyes of his beloved, or anything that would make his beloved think less of him. It therefore inspired a noble code of conduct. Even the opponents of the movement conceded that it produced a highly civilized behavior among its proponents.

The tradition established by the troubadors has been an enduring one. The concept of man being gentle towards the meek and towards women and children exists to this day. "Gentleman" originally meant wellborn, and it was first used by the troubadors to indicate that a person was compassionate towards those in need.

The troubadors gave the Middle Ages a new or at least alternate concept of behavior, in which bravery was combined with gentleness and courtesy. In the Arthurian legend of Camelot we find the slogan "Might for right." Our concept of honor also originates in that time: the notion that one's behavior would be governed by love and not by mercenary motives.

The troubadors were the first to make a virtue of passionate love. Here we find the origins of the deification of romantic love in what we today call Western (predominantly English-speaking) culture. The troubadors introduced to us the idea that intense passionate experience is the purpose of romantic love. Unfortunately, this model is incompatible with another model of our culture: the demand for instant gratification.

## Who Wrote the Book of Love?

The mythology of romantic love as it now exists thus began in an archetypal relationship between a man and a woman of a particular historial group and dominant social class, the courtly society of the twelfth and thirteenth centuries.

While this group has long since been dissolved, curiously, its laws, principles, and beliefs remain our own in an unsuspected and diluted form. Although rationally rejected by a supposedly liberated society, these laws have become the more compelling in that they are the stuff of which our dreams are made. The Western model of romantic love is probably best represented by Shakespeare's *Romeo and Juliet,* by the legend of King Arthur and Camelot, and by the centuries-old stories on which Richard Wagner based his *Tristan und Isolde.*

This myth operates wherever passion is dreamed of as an ideal, and it lives in the fantasies of young girls and boys everywhere, especially in the young girl or boy that still dwells within each one of us. The myth continues to exist in the lives of each of us who thinks that passionate love is stronger and more real than responsibility, society, or morality.

Although the organizing principles we are looking for are contained in Shakespeare's *Romeo and Juliet,* in Arthurian legend, and in the early stories of Tristan and Iseult, we will choose the latter for further exploration, because I feel that the hero, Tristan, is the more archetypal of our modern heroes.

Though at the moment this may seem to you to be no more than an interesting academic side trip, I assure you that a key to retrieving much of our power to be happy lies here. For it is in a model of romantic love that so many of us find imprisonment. Releasing our ability to construct enriched models of relationships is a key to leading richer, more rewarding, and more powerful lives—lives that embody within them the exhilaration and magic that we have come to reserve for those few precious times when we "fall in love." That rare and wonderful experience of the passionate life is available to each of us as part of our daily experiences, but we must first free ourselves from the tyranny of the myths we have inherited. With that in mind, let us explore the organizing principles of this ancient tale.

### Tristan and Iseult, the Original Legend

Tristan, our hero, is born in misfortune. His father has just died and his mother does not survive his birth. King Mark of Cornwall, his mother's brother, takes the orphan into his castle at Tintagel and brings him up there.

As a youth, Tristan performs a feat of physical strength and skill. He vanquishes the Morholt, an Irish giant who has come like a minotaur to claim his tribute of Cornish maidens and youths. The Morholt is killed but not before he has wounded Tristan with a poisoned barb. Having no hope of recovery, Tristan pleads to be put on board a boat that is cast adrift without sail or oar. He takes with him his sword and harp.

He lands in Ireland. There is only one remedy that can save him, and, as it happens, the Queen of Ireland is alone in knowing its secret. But the giant Morholt was this queen's brother, so Tristan is careful not to disclose his name or to explain how he came by his wound. Iseult, the Queen's daughter, nurses him back to health. Tristan returns to Cornwall. So far so good.

A few years later a bird brings to King Mark a golden hair. Seeing this as an omen, the king determines to marry the woman from whose head the hair has come. It is Tristan whom he selects to go in quest of her. A storm causes our hero to be cast ashore once again in Ireland. There he fights and kills a dragon that was threatening to destroy the community. Tristan, having been wounded by the dragon, is again nursed by Iseult.

One day she learns that the wounded stranger is none other than the man who killed her uncle. She seizes Tristan's sword and threatens to kill him. It is then that he tells her the purpose of his mission on behalf of King Mark. Iseult spares him, for she would like to be a queen, and, as she looks into the eyes of Tristan, she finds him especially handsome and promptly falls in love.

Tristan and the Princess set sail for Cornwall. At sea the wind drops and the heat grows oppressive. They are thirsty. Brangaene, Iseult's maid in waiting, gives them a drink. But by mistake she pours out the magic love potion, which the Queen of Ireland, Iseult's mother, has brewed for King Mark and Iseult to share upon the completion of the wedding ceremony. Tristan and Iseult drink it. The result is to commit them to a fate from which they can never escape, for the two are now bound by a transfiguring love—a love that prefers night to day, a love that prefers death to life. They confess that they are now hopelessly in love, and fall into one another's arms.

(Let it be noted here that, according to the archetypal version, the effect of the love potion is limited to three years. In another version, the importance of the love potion is minimized as far as possible, and the love of Tristan and Iseult is depicted as having taken place spontaneously. On the other hand, most of the other versions of the myth attribute unlimited effect to the magic of this drink. Nothing could be more significant than these variations, as we shall presently see.)

Tristan now finds himself between the proverbial rock and hard place. His commitment of love to Iseult represents a betrayal of his king and of the mission with which he has been entrusted. This notwithstanding, Tristan delivers Iseult to King Mark. On the wedding night, Iseult's maid, Brangaene, through an ingenious ruse, takes Iseult's place in the royal bed in order to save her mistress from dishonor and in an attempt to make amends for the irretrievable mistake she made in pouring out the love potion.

The next development in this complex tale has four "felon" (meaning "wicked") barons of the king telling their sovereign that Tristan and Iseult are lovers. Tristan is banished from the castle but, thanks to another ingenious trick, King Mark is convinced of Tristan's innocence and allows his return.

Then Frocin, a dwarf who is in league with the barons, lays a trap in order to establish the lovers' guilt. On the floor around Iseult's bed he scatters flour and persuades King Mark to order Tristan to ride to King Arthur at Carduel upon sunrise the next morning. Tristan feels compelled to embrace his mistress once more before departing. To avoid leaving footmarks in the flour which he has spotted, Tristan performs a long jump onto the queen's bed. But the effort of this display of agility reopens the wound in his leg inflicted the previous day by a boar.

Led by Frocin, the king and the barons inspect Iseult's bed chamber. They find the flour bloodstained. King Mark is satisfied with this evidence of adultery. Iseult is handed over to a party of a hundred lepers, and Tristan is sent to the stake.

On the way to the execution, however, he is allowed to go into a chapel on the side of a cliff. Tristan forces a window and leaps over the cliff to freedom. After he rescues Iseult from the colony of lepers, they go and hide in the depths of the forest of Morrois. There, in the harsh environment of the forest, they live for three years.

One day King Mark, while riding through the forest, discovers the two lovers lying asleep by each other's side. However, before going off to sleep, Tristan had placed his drawn sword between himself and Iseult. King Mark, interpreting the drawn sword as "the sword of chastity"—evidence of the couple's innocence—is moved to pardon them and without waking them he replaces Tristan's sword with his own.

As the three years draw to a close, the potency of the love potion wears off. At this point in the tale, Tristan repents and Iseult wishes that she were queen again. The couple enlist the aid of the hermit Ogrin, through whom Tristan offers his peace to the king and his commitment to surrender Iseult. Mark promises forgiveness.

As the royal procession approaches, the lovers part. However, before their parting, Iseult asks Tristan to stay in the neighborhood until she has determined that King Mark is treating her well. Tristan agrees, and Iseult as a final statement of intrigue declares that she will join him at the first sign he makes. For, she says, nothing shall hold her from doing his bidding.

The two of them meet secretly several times in the hut of Orri, a woodsman. However, the felon barons are keeping the queen's virtue under surveillance. Iseult is apprehended, asks for and is granted a "judgment of God." Before grasping the red-hot iron which will not harm those who speak the truth, Iseult swears that no man has ever held her in his arms except the king and a poor pilgrim who has just carried her ashore from a boat. Of course the poor pilgrim is Tristan in disguise. So, thanks to yet another trick, the ordeal is a success.

A new series of adventures carries Tristan far away from Iseult, so far away that one day he finally assumes that she no longer loves him. Whereupon he agrees to marry, "for her beauty and her name," another Iseult, Iseult "of the white hand." This marriage was not consummated, because Tristan still has his longing for "Iseult the Fair."

As the story draws to a close, Tristan lies dying from wounds inflicted by a poisoned spear. His only chance of survival is if Iseult responds to his request for her presence at his side, for she alone has the power to save his life. She comes, and as her ship draws near, a white sail is hoisted as a sign of hope. But Tristan's wife, who has been on the lookout, and who is tormented by jealousy, runs to Tristan and tells him that the sail is black. Heartbroken, Tristan dies. As he does so, Iseult lands and, on arriving at the castle, lies down beside her dead lover, clutches him close, and promptly also dies.

## End of Story, Beginning of Myth

Upon cool consideration, this classic tale of passion and romance appears of flimsy substance. All of the motives central to the theme of action appear rather inconsequential. Tristan delivers Iseult to the king because he is bound by allegiance of loyalty and duty demanded in the relationship between a knight and his king; at the end of three years spent in the forest, the lovers part because the love potion has lost its potency; Tristan marries Iseult of the White Hand for her beauty and her name. If these reasons are then set aside, the romance turns out to depend upon a series of mystifying contradictions.

At this point you might well ask, "What does all this have to do with the twentieth century in general and the nature of my personal relationships in particular?" Well, let us continue to explore these contradictions, because the plot thickens as we go on, and the answers will become clear.

## A Look at the Contradictions

At the outset of the legend, Tristan is depicted as physically superior to all of his foes and particularly to King Mark. It thus follows that no external power prevents him from carrying off Iseult and thus fulfilling his fate. Indeed, it was the custom of the time to sanction the rights of the stronger—these rights being considered divine and without qualification—especially in the case of a man's rights over a woman. Why in the legend does Tristan not take advantage of these rights?

It seems very strange that thirteenth-century poets and myth-makers, ordinarily fastidious in matters of honor and codes of chivalry, should let pass without a word of comment so much seemingly indefensible behavior.

We must also ask: How can they hold up Tristan as a model of chivalry when he betrays his king with the most shameless cunning, or the queen as a virtuous lady when she is not only an adulteress, but appears not even to think twice before committing an act of blasphemous perjury? On the other hand, why do they call "felons" the four barons who defend King Mark's honor and who, even if motivated by jealousy, neither deceive nor betray, which is more than can be said of Tristan?

The puzzling aspects of this legend continue. Knightly allegiance to the king required that Tristan should deliver to Mark the betrothed he had been sent to fetch. Yet his compliance with this duty seems strange in light of the fact that once he has delivered Iseult he knows no rest until he figures out a way to get back into the castle and betray his knightly code of ethics in an act of adultery.

And about the love potion: If it was brewed specifically for King Mark and his queen, why is its potency not permanent rather than of three years' duration? After all, three years of married bliss are not much. And when Tristan marries another Iseult "for her beauty and her name" but does not consummate this marriage in a sexul union, it seems obvious that nothing has compelled him either to marry or to be guilty of his insulting chastity. Why did he do it?

## The Plot Thickens

All these contradictions begin to resolve if we recognize that the passionate romance of Tristan and Iseult reflects something important that was taking place in the second half of the twelfth century: an evolving antagonism between the rule of chivalry and feudal custom. In this light, perplexing mysteries of the tale begin to make sense. If we examine the stark reality of historical records, it seems likely that the whole charade of romance and courtly chivalry was never more than an ideal. (Remember the definition of "Romantic"—"Having no basis in fact, a fabrication.") The first writers to mention this code commonly lament its decay without noticing that the form they wish it to take has existence only in their dreams.

Moreover, the conflict of some ideal way of living, when contrasted with the harshness of reality, is an essential element of romantic mythology.

The problem with this comes in our acceptance of their dreams as a supposedly attainable reality. Some eight centuries later we pursue their romantic ideal, which remains as incompatible with our modern world as it was with theirs. Remember, we defined insanity as the merger of unworkable illusion with whatever we call reality. There is some place in each of us yearning for our handsome prince (knight) or beautiful princess and an idyllic life.

This would be okay, except we think it should be obtainable and consequently resent our life as in fact it is. The path that returns us to sanity starts with our construction of a new model compatible with reality and in pursuit of which we are nurtured. More about the practical aspects of this later. Meanwhile, back to our myth.

If we accept that Tristan's experience was intended to illustrate a conflict between chivalry and the reality of feudal society—and hence a conflict between two kinds of duty and, furthermore, between two conflicting orders of morality—then it becomes possible to make a number of the episodes of the tale intelligible.

Customs change with time, and by the middle of the twelfth century an Arthurian knight, such as Tristan, exactly like a troubador of the south, regarded himself as the vassal of some chosen Lady, when actually he remained the vassal of a Lord. This gives rise to a number of conflicting claims which are played out in this tale of romance and tragic passion.

Let us return to the riddle of the four "felon" barons. According to feudal morality, it was the duty of a vassal (knight) to warn his lord of anything that might endanger the latter's rights or honor. In fact, he was a "felon" if he did not. Now in the tale of Tristan and Iseult the barons go and tell King Mark how Iseult is behaving. They should, therefore, be considered faithful and true. If, then, the author of the myth refers to them as "felons," he must evidently do so on the basis of some other moral code: the code of chivalry. For according to a well-quoted judgment delivered by the Gascon Courts of Love: Whosoever discloses the secrets of a courtly love is a felon.

Apparently then, the various authors of the romance of Tristan and Iseult are deliberately siding with "courtly chivalry" against common law.

The notion that romantic passion carries us to a reality in which we are no longer bound by the laws of mortal men survives to this day. We can find case after case of ruined lives belonging to individuals who ran afoul of social decency and common law, as they relentlessly pursued the object of their passion. Inevitably, when apprehended they believe their behavior to be justified and seem amazed that others "just don't understand." An alarmingly high percentage of homicides are "justified" in the name of passionate love.

In addition, the view of fidelity and of marriage that was adopted in the courtly love of the mid-twelfth century influences our behavior today and offers further explanation of the striking contradictions of the tale. According to official historical theory, courtly love and its attendant codes of conduct arose as a reaction to the brutal lawlessness of feudal life.

## Love and Marriage Go Together
## Like a Horse and Roller Skates

It is well known that the nobles of the twelfth century made marriage simply a means of enriching themselves, either through the annexation of dower estates or through expectations of inheritance. When a deal (marriage) turned out badly, the wife was repudiated. Such repudiation generally took the form of entering the plea that the relationship had been discovered as incestuous, and in the face of this the laws of the Church prohibiting divorce were powerless. To allege consanguinity of even the fourth degree, no matter on what slender evidence, was enough to secure an annulment of the marriage.

In order to counteract these abuses, which led to frequent quarreling and to wars, courtly love established a fidelity and allegiance that was independent of legal marriage and of which the sole basis was love. It was even contended, in the famous judgment delivered by a court of love in the house of the Countess of Champagne, that love and marriage were incompatible. The judgment reads as follows:

We declare and affirm, by the tenor of these present, that love cannot extend its rights over two married persons. For indeed lovers grant one another all things mutually and freely, without being impelled by any motive of necessity, whereas husband and wife are held by their duty to submit their wills to each other and to refuse each other nothing.

May this judgment which we have delivered with extreme caution, and after consulting with a great number of other ladies, be for you a constant and unassailable truth, delivered in this year 1174, on the third day before the Kalends of May, proclamation VII.

If this belief is shared by both Tristan and the authors of the romance, the sense given to the terms "felony" and "adultery" is thereby justified—indeed more than justified, exalted, since it implies an unshakable loyalty to the higher law of courtly love.

The legend misses no opportunity to deprecate the social institution of marriage and to humiliate husbands, in this case, the aging King Mark, who was always so easily deceived. At the same time, the legend glorifies the virtue of men and women who love outside of and in spite of marriage.

This courtly love, however, displays a curious feature. It appears to be opposed to the satisfaction of love as much as it is to marriage. The prevailing attitude of the Arthurian knight was to pledge fidelity and love without ever fully possessing his Lady, for whatever turned into the reality of possession could no longer remain the idealized model of courtly love. In the light of this, we can find the explanation of such episodes as that of the Sword of Chastity, of Iseult's return to her king after staying in the forest of Morrois, and even of Tristan's marriage to Iseult of the White Hand.

In modern times, our claim of passion would require Tristan to carry off Iseult as soon as he and she had drunk the love potion. They should then live happily ever after. Instead, he delivers her to King Mark, and he does so because the model of courtly love did not allow a passion of this kind to turn into a reality, as this would result in the "full possession of his Lady." Therefore, Tristan chooses to respect the law of feudal allegiance, which is then used to incite the romance according to courtly ideal. We must note that Tristan chooses to do so quite freely, because, given his physical superiority with respect to the king and the barons and given the custom of the time, he could have resorted to the right of force.

Rationally it is a strange love indeed that conforms to laws by which it stands condemned in order to better preserve itself!

### Is It "Only a Myth"?

At this point, it is of course tempting to claim that this is only a myth and that all of the external barriers to the fulfillment of Tristan's love are only fictional inventions. None of which, we can say, has anything to do with our twentieth-century relationships. We must remember, however, that at this time in history the process of acquiring wisdom made extensive use of the legendary metaphor as passed on by accomplished storytellers.

This situation did not radically change until the fifteenth century, when Johann Gutenberg, a German printer, initiated a revolution in the acquisition of knowledge with the invention of movable type.

We are, therefore, justified in paying more attention to this tale of romantic passion than we would otherwise be tempted to. For it is through legends such as this that moral standards were communicated and preserved. In the seemingly capricious and arbitrary nature of the obstructions introduced into this story we will discover the essence of the passion with which it is concerned.

### What Is the Legend Really About?

What, then, is the legend of Tristan and Iseult really about? We could take the point of view that the story seems to be about the partings of the lovers, because it is not too much to say that they never miss a chance of getting parted. Indeed, when there is no obstruction, they invent one. These partings are enacted in the name of passion, so that in separation their love may be intensified and transfigured, all of this at the cost of their happiness and eventually their lives. Now the hidden and disturbing significance of the myth is beginning to loom.

Often it has been noted that only "foolish" questions can enlighten us, for behind whatever seems obvious lies something that is not. Let us then be obvious and ask: Does Tristan care for Iseult and she for him? After all, the lovers do not seem to be brought together in any normal *human* way. It may seem that their relationship at the outset consisted of the relationship between the wounded and the healer, and was the embodiment of what is human in character, but there is magic at work. We must remember that the Morholt's dart carried a witch's poison and that the Queen of Ireland makes available through her daughter, Iseult, the magical antidote by way of which Tristan is saved.

When the two meet again under similar circumstances, Iseult, upon discovering the details of Tristan's past, promptly wants to kill him. In fact, upon close examination of the detailed account of the legend, all evidence suggests that the two would never have chosen one another were they acting *freely*.

If we set aside Wagner's liberties with the original version of the tale, it is not until they drink the love potion that passion flares between them. That any human fondness unites them is never indicated. Indeed, we find indications to the contrary, as the full text describes the lovers' two visits to the hermit Ogrin.

The first time they go to see him, they do so to make a confession. But instead of confessing their sins and asking for absolution, they do their utmost to convince Ogrin that they are not to blame for what has come to pass, since, after all, *they do not care for one another!* Specifically, Tristan protests, "If she loves me, it is by the poison which holds me from leaving her and her from leaving me." And continues Iseult, "Lord, by almighty God, he loves me not, nor I him; except for an herb potion which I drank and which he drank, it was a sin." Alas, they are protrayed as absolute victims of passionate love.

Thus presented, the two are trapped in a bittersweet paradox. They love passionately, but not one another.

On the one hand, they have sinned, but on the other hand, they cannot repent, for they are not to blame. They make a confession but desire neither reform nor forgiveness. In the grand tradition of all great lovers, they imagine that they have been forcibly carried beyond good and evil into a kind of transcendental state outside ordinary human experience, into a realm at odds with the world but which they feel to be more real than the world.

### It's Not Just "Bigger than Both of Us," It's Bigger than All of Us

The couple are depicted as being prisoners of an exquisite anquish as a result of a series of magical events which neither of them controls. Their perception of their circumstance is further revealed in their conversation with Ogrin. Warns Ogrin:

"Love by force dominates you."
"How long will your folly last?"
"Too long you have been leading this life."
Responds Tristan:
"Now harken, if for long we have been leading this life, that is because it was our destiny."

We can only conclude as a result of all this that, in fact, Tristan and Iseult do not love one another. Indeed, they say they don't, and everything goes to demonstrate this. *In actuality what they love is love and being in love*. Their behavior reflects that it is their belief that whatever obstructs love must inflame and preserve it. As an obstruction approaches insurmountability, their passion seemingly approaches an infinite intensity.

Tristan loves the passion of loving far more than he loves Iseult the Fair. In reality Iseult does nothing to hold Tristan, for all she needs is her passionate dream. Their need of one another is merely a means to an end: to be impassioned. They do not need each other as they are. What they need is not each other's presence, but each other's absence. The partings of the lovers are dictated by the organizing principle of their passion itself. That is why the Romance abounds in obstructions and why events work up in a romantic climax to a glorified and fatal ideal. In seeking the ultimate obstacle, unaware and in spite of themselves, the lovers have pursued the single goal of death.

We can now begin to see why Eros was feared in Greek times. Neither man nor gods were immune from his influence. If struck by his barb, one was transported beyond morality, reason, and responsibility. Under this influence one was likely to repudiate all those things previously made important. All this in pursuit of the object of one's passion.

It evidences itself also in the legend of the Round Table. Lancelot's passionate love for Guinevere together with King Arthur's one night of passion with his sister (which produced his son Mordred) resulted in the downfall of an entire society which had been built upon Arthur's enlightened idealism. So, romantic and passionate love has always been presented in our culture as a harbinger of tragic social consequences, a prelude to pain, conflict, suffering, and death.

This notion of death as a goal of passionate lovers may seem a little hard to swallow, but it must be remembered that eight centuries later Freud advanced his theory that "the goal of all life is death." Freud further maintained that the essence of man consists, not as Descartes maintained, in thinking, but in desiring. Furthermore, while we might be consciously aware of our thoughts, we are almost never consciously aware of our true desires.

Western tradition has evolved to maintain that the goal of mankind is to become as contemplative as possible. To quote Descartes: "I think, therefore I am." Freudian psychology, on the other hand, eliminates the category of pure contemplation as nonexistent. Only a wish, says Freud, can possibly set our mind in motion. Desire, he maintained, is the essence of man, desire in this case being defined as energy directed towards the procurement of pleasure and the avoidance of pain.

In the words of Freud, "Our entire physical activity is bent upon procuring pleasure and avoiding pain. It is automatically regulated by the pleasure principle." Or, "It is simply the pleasure principle which draws up the program of life's purpose." This idea does not imply any particular theory as to the sources of pleasure. It is an idea taken from common sense and runs parallel to Aristotle's dictum that all men seek happiness. Freud maintains that the goal of the pleasure principle is happiness.

The problem that now presents itself may be stated as follows: Man's desire for happiness is in conflict with reality. What we have come to call reality imposes on humankind a series of frustrating limitations to the realization of the pleasure principle. This conflict, this ongoing frustration, is the cause of the repression that provides a source of neurosis that leads to the dictum that "all men are mad."

With this last statement I have for many years concurred. Often I have smiled at the thought that this planet Earth may in fact be the insane asylum of the galaxy. However, we must press on, for to state a problem without advancing a way out is of little service.

## Why We Can't Make Love Stay

What drives *us* crazy is that we seek to be the effect of circumstances that are pleasurable and instead we seem constantly the effect of circumstances that are painful. History—the biography of human neurosis—is a series of horror stories. Since the beginning of time, humankind has been ravaged by plagues, wars, and famines. Sadly, human history becomes a tribute to what we can survive in spite of and still learn nothing from.

It is perhaps impossible for those of us who have not lived through such devastating catastrophes to conceive of the lasting impact such events have on the human mind and spirit. Even a small appreciation of the horrors of the past explains people's preoccupation with the avoidance of pain. We are continually organizing ourselves around the motive of the avoidance of loss. And at the same time we relentlessly pursue the objects of our imagined pleasure.

Returning to the legend of Tristan and Iseult, we find two components of the tale that demand further explanation. They are the irresponsibility of the lovers and the principle that lies behind their continued parting. Though it has become fashionable to suppose that we human beings are naturally irresponsible, I am certain that this is not the case. Our interpretation of past events conspires with the programming of the established order to convince us that we live in a world in which we are helpless, inadequate, and totally incapable of self-nourishment on any spiritual, emotional, or material level. But, tragically, what appears to be true acquires power over us, regardless of whether or not it is actually true.

If we believe that we are not responsible, we will behave as if we have nothing to do with what happens to us. We will live as if the origins of our pain and of our pleasure are completely external to us. We will see ourselves as victims of a chaotic world that is uncaring and devoid of justice.

Tristan and Iseult, in the vernacular of contemporary popularized psychology, would certainly be described as possessing a *victim consciousness*. While we can justifiably argue that the events of the story do conspire to create a reality in the lovers' minds that they are victims, and that the events of history conspire to create in the minds of all of us that we are victims, it is essential that we recognize that we do not have to be seduced by this conspiracy. When, in our model of reality, we are the victim of life, then the only solution to life is death.

The consequences of a model of reality in which we see ourselves as a victim of life leave us floundering in the double bind we have explored before. Remember, it is the nature of our human organism that continued exposure or involvement in that which we seem the effect of will reduce the degree of the effect. We build tolerance, assuming of course that we survive the initial effects!

This important principle is revealed in our relationship to infectious diseases. New disease strains when introduced to a population initially may carry high fatality rates. It is not generally recognized, for instance, that common childhood diseases such as measles, chickenpox, and mumps were originally fatal diseases. Considered from the viewpoint of military logistics, the Spanish conquest of Mexico appears as impossible fiction. How could Hernán Cortés, starting off with about six hundred men, conquer the Aztec Empire, whose population numbered millions? How could such a tiny force of strangers, far from home, in an alien land, prevail against these odds?

The riddle is without any satisfactory answer until we discover that the Spaniards carried with them disease strains to which they had become immune but which were lethal to the previously unexposed Aztec population. These people became the victims on a mass scale of the common childhood diseases of Europe. The results were catastrophic. In less than fifty years, the population of central Mexico had collapsed from approximately twenty-five or thirty million to about three million. With the passage of time the Amerindian population of Mexico developed a level of tolerance to these diseases. In other words, with continued exposure, what was once fatal became a minor irritation.

Another good example is the spread of the black

death in Europe. In mid-fourteenth century the plague
reduced the population of Europe by approximately
one third. Indeed, some communities ceased to exist.
The final death toll is estimated at twenty million. The
disease was carried by fleas that infested the rat population. Today, most of the ground-burrowing animal
population of Northern California and their fleas also
carry the plague. Here again the passage of time has
allowed us to develop a level of tolerance that renders
this fact no longer a threat. While this may seem far
removed from our discussion of passionate love, it
isn't as we shall presently see. Because this kind of
tolerance represents the good news. Now comes the
bad news.

If we return to the idea that the essence of man is
directed towards the procurement of pleasure and the
avoidance of pain, having established that prolonged
exposure to that which we are the effect of results in a
decrease in the intensity of the effect, we are face to
face with the bad news as it applies to passionate love.
Togetherness builds tolerance whereby the intensity of
passion is destroyed. Here is the double bind, of
passionate love and the principle at work behind the
constant parting of the lovers Tristan and Iseult.

A model of reality in which we are not responsible
or accountable for our emotions, our feelings, and our
actions is implicit in the mythology of passionate love.
In the legend of Tristan and Iseult we have examined
the evidence of the lovers' convictions that, by reason
of the love potion, they cannot be held accountable for
their situation or the resultant events. As we step back
into the twentieth century, an abundance of similar
messages can be found in our mediums of popular
music, film, and drama. From early twentieth-century
America we select the following song, archetypal in its
nature and well known to us all:

You made me love you. I didn't want to do it.
I didn't want to do it.

You made me want you. And all the time you
knew it.
And all the time you knew it.
You made me happy sometimes. You made me
glad.
But there were times, dear, you made me feel so
bad . . . *

This sounds like an update of Tristan and Iseult's
conversation with Ogrin, the hermit! Even the expression "falling in love" implies an absence of responsibility for the events that will follow.

For those who have "fallen in love" the dilemma
may be summarized as follows: Falling in love is the
experience of being exquisitely and exhilaratingly the
effect of the person with whom we claim to have fallen
in love. Since we find this situation initially delicious,
and since we think we know a good thing when we
taste it, we immediately assume the status of an ad-
dict. We want as much as we can get. The problem is,
however, as is the case with any addiction, that more
of the same does not produce more of the same
experience. To the contrary—*more of the same results
in less of the same experience!*

In our ecstasy we are as little children and, in
accordance with Freud's theory, demand endless rep-
etition of what we consider to be the cause of our
pleasure. Unfortunately, the principle of endless rep-
etition doesn't work. The expected intensity of experience is not forthcoming and leads to—often
unconsciously—a level of resentment out of which
emerges "the quarrels of lovers."

Here we have defined the classic double bind. We
actively seek pleasure and avoid pain. We find an
exquisite source of pleasure—our beloved—and we
want as much as we can get. If we get as much as we

---

*"You Made Me Love You—I Didn't Want to Do It," words by Joe McCarthy, music by
James V. Monaco.

think we want, the degree of our ecstasy is diminished, to be replaced by the feelings of fear and the pain of loss. If it is our nature to pursue pleasure and avoid pain and if the repeated pursuit of a discovered pleasure is in effect *the pursuit of pain,* then we are indeed in a situation from which only death appears to offer an escape.

Now the partings of Tristan and Iseult can be well understood. So too can the fear with which Eros and his handiwork have been traditionally regarded. In essence, this popularly existing model of passion and romantic love can lead only to frustration, conflict, suffering, and some form of death.

Romantic love in the reality we have constructed is like a flower that has been picked and put in a vase. No matter how beautiful it is at the moment, it is destined soon to wither and die.

Legend would have us know that once passionate love is consummated, it too is destined to wither and die. Here we are told that the only way to keep passion alive is never to allow its consummation. The way to keep it is never to have it. This is the message implicit in the detailed and endless accounts of obstacles to love and the frequent partings of lovers. We are never offered a detailed account of love's labor won.

While nineteenth-century Romantic poets and novelists would have us believe in a happy-ever-after, notice we never followed Cinderella and the handsome Prince beyond the point at which they walked up the palace steps and closed the door behind them.

But we do know what happened to them. We have tried to live behind the closed door. We have the dubious honor of living in a culture that has attained the form of its most treasured dreams, only to find them empty of experience.

We have painfully discovered that almost every relationship that begins with a rush of passionate bliss winds up in some state of boredom or conflict. We become immune to being the passionate effect of our beloved. We, of course, interpret this as a divine message from the Creator to split, which we do, only to start the whole charade all over again.

So here we are, in a grand predicament. We glorify and pursue passion, without which life is a mundane series of colorless, predictable events. Sudden passion, "falling in love," gives new meaning to life, lifting us beyond the realm of ordinary reality. We are, for the moment, actually happy. We are saved. We are free. But then we become fearful, because we know that this happiness, like an orgasm, cannot be sustained.

The result is only more of the pain that we as humanity so desperately try to avoid. Except this time it's an existential pain, one that cannot be ignored. After all, we are the generation that has everything you are supposed to have for life not to hurt, and life still hurts.

The only way we can seemingly escape the pain is to become less and less aware, to lower our consciousness to the point below which we do not perceive the pain. So we pursue oblivion to forget our pain, at the cost of our power, at the cost of our happiness and, finally, of our life.

This is the human dilemma; this is the legacy left us by our forebears. This is the unwinnable game that we have been born into the middle of. Notice that the Declaration of Independence guarantees us the right to the "Pursuit of Happiness" but does not guarantee its attainment.

Clearly, we must find a way out of this labyrinth of neurosis and free ourselves from the living death of our inherited emotional wilderness. Even as romantic love seems to leave us abandoned in this labyrinth of disillusionment and pain, it is another love that leads us to freedom for happiness.

Nothing will change until we recognize that our passion must transcend the condition of being an effect. We must grow beyond the idea that the other person is doing it to us, and realize that we can create a passionate experience which is beyond romance and has a basis in fact.

The passionate experience isn't up to them; it's up to us. We have to consciously, imaginatively, magically create the passionate life. To do this requires wisdom, style, *savoir faire,* and great artistry. To have a consciously passionate relationship requires the kind of artistry that made Picasso Picasso and da Vinci da Vinci. Great artists are great lovers of the passionate experience of life.

We cannot enjoy the benefits of great artistry if we have not applied ourselves to the joyful and exquisite discipline of becoming a great artist and lover of life.

This is the subject matter of the next chapter.

# 14

## Conscious Love

It is through the mastery of the principles of conscious love that we will come to know and experience the magnificence of the human spirit and the full beauty of life. Conscious love becomes the ongoing celebration of our relationship with the spiritual reality of life. It is the love that provides for the creative and continuing passionate experience.

We will start with a definition.

**Conscious love has as its motive the impassioned desire that the object fully actualize its own inherent perfection, independent of the consequences to the lover. It is a state of service.**

Let us now take some time to go over this definition and make it useful to us.

The word "conscious" means knowing, with awareness; it means to be aware of oneself as a thinking being, knowing what one is doing and why. Obviously, then, we cannot "fall in" conscious love! It is not some kind of effect or something that simply happens to us, rather it is something we choose to create. This is a beautiful idea, because we cannot be hurt by what we know we are creating.

The word "love" means literally a deep and tender feeling of affection for; a feeling of brotherhood and good will; a strong interest in. We find here in Webster's definition the ideas inherent in the Greek word "agape," which coincides with the meaning we have previously given to the term "instinctual love." Notice that there is nothing implicitly romantic, passionate, or sexual in the definition of the word "love."

The word "motive" means "some inner drive or intention." Throughout this book we have continually referred to the principle that all behavior reinforces the motivating idea behind the behavior, and this remains true with conscious love. In our past we have been, for the most part, reinforcing our motives unconsciously, i.e., unintentionally. The fact that this process has been both unconscious and unintentional has not spared us the painful consequences of the destructive aspects of this process.

Now we have the opportunity to have this principle absolutely work for us. In our pursuit of conscious love, our behavior will now reinforce our conscious inner drive and intention. As we develop awareness and consciously choose our behavior to actualize creative intentions, we develop more and more personal power.

The phrase "impassioned desire" denotes a strong inner drive demanding external expression.

The word in our definition that may seem out of place is the word "object." However, this word has been chosen with great care. Let's repeat the definition up to this point. "Conscious love has as its motive the impassioned desire that the OBJECT . . . " The purpose of using the word object here, rather than a word like "beloved," is to give us a little jolt that reminds that a suitable recipient of our conscious love need not be limited to human form.

Here once more we have an important idea. As I sit typing this chapter my family sits watching a public broadcasting television program that seeks to inform us about the damage we are inflicting on the environment. Our earthly environment is in urgent need of our conscious love.

Another suitable recipient of our conscious love is our work. As I meet and study people whose lives are rich and full and happy, I inevitably find that these are people who have a passion for the work they do. Freud has told us that a healthy person can love and work. It is a sad reality indeed—if the surveys are to be believed—that 80 percent of Americans who work do so at jobs they dislike. When we consider we spend more of our waking hours at work than we do in our relationship, to not love our work is a terrible waste of a major part of our life.

If we look for an expression of conscious love that has endured through the ages, we find it most readily in the field of art. When you feast your eyes on the inspirational works of Michelangelo, you are a witness to the fruits of conscious love. A man or a woman does not create works of art that reflect exquisite beauty and purity of spirit, other than as an expression of conscious love.

I feel most strongly that we must seek out a field in which to work that provides us with an avenue for our expression of ourselves in a way that we know makes a positive difference to others and to the world around us. This is an essential element of a rich and happy life. The evidence is clear that those of us who find more outlets for our creative self-expression than we have hours in the day to use them, live healthier and longer lives.

Back to our definition: "Conscious love has as its motive the impassioned desire that the object fully actualize its own inherent perfection . . ." The word actualize means to make real through action, a process we keep stressing throughout this book. The best information and great realizations become valuable only when we act on them. In fact, we don't know anything we don't live in action. If our fear is to leave us and be replaced by the experience of mastery, power, and love, we must take action, as these experiences can be made real only through action.

The word "perfection" is a very beautiful word, and generally its meaning is misunderstood. Most of us respond to the word with ambivalence. On the one hand, we want our lives to be perfect, and on the other hand, we feel intimidated by the expectations that we believe are placed upon us to be perfect. A look in Webster will begin to straighten things out. The definition reads as follows: "per.fect, to finish 1. complete in all respects; without defect or omission; sound; flawless 2. in a condition of complete excellence; . . . pure; utter; sheer; absolute."

Did you just get intimidated again? Don't worry, this is going to turn out okay.

All of the intimidating aspects of the word disappear once we realize that we can only perfectly be ourselves. We can't perfectly be anybody else. When the prophet Joshua was preparing for death, the people wondered what questions he thought God would ask him. Said Joshua: "He will not ask me why I was not God, He will ask me why I was not Joshua."

Perfection is not about your being compared to somebody else, or somebody else's standards for you. If we pursue perfection in ourselves this quest is about our being all that we can be. This quest is about our becoming all that we inherently are as a human being. The term "inherent" implies that which is already within us. The spirit of perfection is not competitive; if you see perfection as a competitive term, this is not perfection. Nature has lessons for us here. A rose is always what it is; we do not expect it to be a daffodil.

Think of yourself as a work of art in progress. You will find that this is a very beautiful idea; so think of yourself as a work of art in progress. You will like it.

Back to our definition. "Conscious love has as its motive the impassioned desire that the object fully actualize its own inherent perfection, *independent of the consequences to the lover.*" This last clause we are going to be talking about for a while.

Tragically, the words "I love you" have almost become a threat. We've all had the experience of being in a relationship in which we're having a good time. We continue enjoying each other until the other says, "I love you." Almost always, our immediate reaction will be, "Oh dear, now I'm in trouble." But why? To answer this question let's look at how we've used the words "I love you" in the past.

Those of us who are men can recall an occasion when we said, "I love you," in order to entice someone to do something that we didn't think she would be willing to do if we did not utter these words in a reasonably convincing manner. And I'm sure that women are not without their own way of using the three little words "I love you" for similar purposes.

Our models of sexual reality have resulted in the words "I love you" becoming a laundry detergent. We utter these words in an attempt to make sex clean instead of dirty. If we say we love each other, sex becomes sanitized and is now called "making love." If, on the other hand, we are simply into lust, having sex is somehow dirty.

And how often do we behave in a way that is totally inconsiderate of another and attempt to handle the situation by assuring this person that we "love" him or her? We use the phrase "but I love you" to justify all manner of behavior we wouldn't dream of exhibiting in the presence of someone whose friendship we were trying to cultivate. In fact, we have been known to behave towards those we claim to love in ways we would not towards our avowed enemies!

It is such a pity that the statement "I love you" is so often a prelude to aggression. But this is the case, for example, when the statement is "I love you" and the intended consequence is "now you're going to make me happy." Sometimes the word "love" becomes a prelude to our attempt to possess the person we claim that we love. We say to that person, "I love you," and immediately open an escrow with the intent of gaining full title to his or her life.

When we talk about conscious love, we're talking about loving a person, or our work, or our earth, or anything at all, without allowing the consequences of love to be the motivating force behind our love. This doesn't mean that there won't be consequences for us, because obviously there are going to be consequences and they are likely to be very beautiful.

Some of us have had a taste of loving the earth consciously when we garden and have found the consequences to be wonderful.

In fact, the experience of gardening may have provided us with our most moving experience of the nature of life itself and of relationship with a spiritual reality. Some of us do consciously love our work, and we experience, as a consequence, those moments when our work is magical, truly creative, and a beautiful expression of who we are.

Thus, we are in no way suggesting that we cannot enjoy the most wonderful consequences of conscious love. In fact, we are talking about enjoying the miraculous consequences on a regular basis. What we are saying is that the consequences cannot be the motivating force behind the focus of our conscious love. This is very different from the way most of us operate much of the time, wherein we do what we do because of what we think we are going to get out of it.

The eastern Yogis and Zen masters talk about
sweeping the floor to get the floor clean. Mostly we
don't sweep the floor to get the floor clean; we sweep
the floor because if we don't sweep the floor and get it
clean, somebody will punish us, or we won't get our
pocket money or our paycheck. Here our motivation is
a fear of the consequences of not taking the action of
sweeping the floor. Since we now know that all behavior reinforces the motivating idea behind the behavior,
we can see in this instance that sweeping the floor will
reinforce the level of fear we experience and prevent
us deriving any joy, or even satisfaction, from the
activity.

On the other hand, we have all had the experience of
sweeping the floor or cleaning the bathroom for no
other purpose than to simply get them clean, and we
find ourselves filled with satisfaction and high in spirits
as we survey a perfect result.

I remember talking once to George Lois, an advertising art director of impressive talent, about experiences from his childhood that he felt had contributed
to his outstanding success in his field.

George reminisced that he used to like to lie in bed
on Saturday mornings, but his mother would always
arrive at some ridiculously early hour and begin to
vacuum the carpet in his room. At the time George
was absolutely convinced that his mother did this
simply to irritate him. Additionally, he felt that this
was her attempt to ensure that he did not grow up
without a generous helping of guilt as a part of his
personality.

One day George simply asked his mother why she
was vacuuming the floor. And she answered simply,
"To get it clean."

George recalled that he sat up in bed, stunned by the
recognition that this was the truth. She, in fact, was
vacuuming the floor to get the floor clean, and early
Saturday morning was the time that she had set aside
to do that. She didn't expect that George should start

vacuuming the floor himself, nor did she require him to feel guilty because she was doing it.

George went on to relate that his father had similar qualities. He talked of going to work with his father in the family flower shop in a busy section of New York City. Early in the morning, he would stand alongside his father, removing the thorns from the stems of the roses. George said that when he began to do this work he did it just to get it finished, and while he was doing it he would be preoccupied not only with finishing but with avoiding pricking himself.

His father, on the other hand, would simply stand there removing the thorns with an ease and grace that was beautiful to watch. He would say to George, "Don't do the work to finish the work, just do the work to take off the thorns. Then it will go much faster and your hands will remain unscathed."

As I pause here, for a moment, to review my own life, I clearly see that my moments of greatest happiness come from passionate involvement in my work, when I am doing it just to be doing it. Of course, there are additional consequences of great benefit.

As I go through my life I find myself constantly recalling Plato's statement that it is the essence of man to seek a suitable recipient for his love. This is such an important idea.

I was conducting a workshop the other night for graduates of the Actualizations Workshop and their friends, and a woman who was a friend of a graduate asked the question: "What do we do as adults to overcome the fact that when we were children our parents never gave us all the love they should have?"

I hear this question so often. When I do television shows and there is a chance for viewers to call in with questions, this question is inevitably asked. It is a popular belief that much of our unhappiness is a result of our not being given vast amounts of love when we were children.

*This is not the source of our unhappiness. Even if we*

*were unloved, this is still not the source of our unhap-
piness.*

The true source of our unhappiness is that the love
we had within us as children was not received by
others, others, in this case, usually being our parents.

For us to be truly happy, we must experience that
we are loving, we must love consciously, and we must
experience that our love is received and that it makes a
difference.

Imagine that we live in a world in which we all
believe that we must be loved if we are to be happy.
Imagine, therefore, that we are all rushing around
desperately seeking to be loved. If we are all desperately seeking to be loved, who then is available to do
any of the loving?

On the other hand, simply to be loving is not enough
either. As a matter of fact, the most intense unhappiness that most of us ever experience stems from
unrequited love. The experience of loving another
passionately without this love being either received or
returned has driven many a soul to the depths of
despair. (Although we should add that such love is
seldom, if ever, conscious, and would be better described as a psychotic episode.)

So the task before us is to experience our love, to
offer it consciously, to have it received, and to see that
it makes a positive difference.

It is our mastery of the art of conscious love that can
alone bring us the experience of real and durable
happiness. This love is the answer whence all other
answers to the world's ills must come.

But conscious love is rare.

## Why Is Conscious Love So Rare?

Conscious love is rare because in our impoverished
model of reality we are looking to be loved rather than
to be loving. If you look within your own experience,

you will find that you like yourself best when you love or care for someone or something and you can see that in this way you make a difference. Remember, however, as you seek to be loving, that you can expect that those whom you seek to love will sometimes find it difficult to receive your love. They are likely to possess an impoverished model of reality in which they see themselves as being unworthy of love, yours or anybody else's, for that matter. It will become easier for them to accept yours as they begin to see that you are simply loving them to love them, and that you don't expect *any consequences*.

Your love for them is simply a reflection of your desire that they become able to receive love and use its power to heal and enrich their lives. Your conscious love has as its motive the impassioned desire that this person fully actualize his or her own inherent perfection.

Introduce this person to the idea that he or she is a work of art in progress, and you will find him or her more able to receive you.

Conscious love is also rare because we seldom, if ever, conceive of perfection as an end product or consequence of love. As we grow in consciousness towards enlightenment, we will find revealed the truth, the beauty, and the perfection of life—life's sorrows notwithstanding.

The model of perfection that we have introduced in this chapter is an enlightening purpose. As you travel down the path of this purpose you will discover and experience that there is truth, beauty, and orderliness in the world, and your own life will become rich as you develop the kind of power that heals the ills around you.

But, most of all, conscious love is rare because it demands that we be conscious. The first implication of this is obviously that you cannot "fall into" conscious love. To love consciously is a process of constant choice and ongoing intent. In other words, it is not something that happens to us; rather, it is something that we cause to happen within us and use to illuminate whatever we select as the object of our love.

Since conscious love has as its motive the impassioned desire that the object fully actualize its own inherent perfection, we run into another difficulty that results in conscious love being rare. Namely, we seldom, if ever, really know what is good for the people we love, even if we really want to. Consequently, conscious love requires our discovery of what, in fact, supports the best interests of whom or whatever we claim that we love.

This will require a good deal of exploration on our part. Here a further difficulty arises: We have been trained to use our rational mind in problem-solving, but the rational mind is unsuited to the process of exploration that we are talking about. We must explore instead through the use of our creative, intuitive, inductive, and mystical mind. This brings to us a very deep level of knowing that transcends all rational understanding.

We urgently need to discover, through this process, what will support ourselves, others, and the earth that we share in the revelation of all inherent perfection.

In contrast, mostly we have discovered only how to support each other's limitations. We may do this "lovingly," i.e., with good intent, but the results are still disastrous. How often do we find ourselves making the comment that so and so is "that kind of person," which adds to the agreement that creates the reality that he or she is in fact that kind of person. This is supporting the limitations of the person in question.

For years and years, I managed to get everybody to agree with me that I was a physical klutz. I had the absolute belief that I was a klutz. I behaved in a way that reflected my belief, so everybody agreed that I was a klutzy kind of person, which of course further reinforced my impoverished model of my physical potential.

Anyhow, one day a marvelous woman gets me to go roller-skating. Joanna makes me an offer I can't refuse as she tells me we are going roller-skating. I live in Marin County in California, and the county has thoughtfully provided a walking, jogging, roller-skating trail that winds its way along the bayshore. So I put on the roller skates and I suppose I travel one hundred and fifty feet when a little black boy comes whizzing along.

He shouts, "Hey, mister, it's your first time, isn't it?" I said, "Yep!" He says, "Well, you're doing great!" And I say, "Thanks!" Then he says, "And you know what's great, mister? You're having a terrific time! Big people don't usually have a terrific time doing what they ain't good at!"

This little boy was just loving me. How marvelous it was that this seven-year-old had not yet given up trying to give away love. This is very unusual. Upon arrival on this earth, children are not clambering for love. Rather they have all this love, along with a lot of joy and creativity, and they are very magically saying to the world, "Here, have some, have some."

As adults, we become cool, or at least we try to be cool. I say if you want to be cool, die! But if you want to be alive, you should be as little children. This doesn't mean childish; rather, it means recultivating within you the childlike ability to be filled with wonder as you journey through life.

How often do you catch yourself getting agreement on your own limitations or giving agreement to other people on their limitations?

I had a great time roller-skating that day, and I wouldn't have gone if Joanna had supported my limitations, and I doubt that I would have had as much fun if it had not been for the love and enthusiasm of that little boy.

As a matter of fact, as I began to share with some friends—who I know love me—that I had gone roller-skating, I got the response: "Stewart, I don't think you ought to do that—you tend to be a klutz and you'll probably kill yourself if you continue roller-skating." Of course, they didn't want me to kill myself because they love me, but in the name of love, they were killing another part of me instead (but they can only do this with my permission, which I withheld).

Conscious love demands that we no longer support the imagined limitations, the biases, the narrowness and fear in which we all become imprisoned. We must transcend our inner limits. The challenge of exploring the outer space of the universe pales before the challenge of exploring the inner space of the human species.

I hope that little boy I met roller-skating makes it all the way to adulthood with his ability to love and be alive still intact. The odds aren't great. I am afraid he will be told, "Don't speak to strangers," or, "If you're nice to people they will step all over you," and believe it.

I remember a man in an Actualizations Workshop who stood up and announced that he was going to leave the workshop. I asked, "Jeff, why are you going to leave?" He replied, "Yamma yamma yamma yamma." And I said, "No, Jeff, that isn't why you're going to leave."

I knew full well why Jeff was going to leave, and finally Jeff found the courage within himself to tell the truth about his reason for wanting to leave the workshop.

It turned out that Jeff was sent by his company, which is a major American corporation. They sent Jeff to check us out. They figured if the workshop could get to Jeff, then it had to work. Jeff was their resident rock.

So Jeff stood up and let us know that he came to the workshop thinking that he would simply be an observer. However, he began to discover that you cannot be in the presence of one hundred people who are searching for ways to support their own and each

other's inherent perfection without becoming personally involved.

Jeff commented that he couldn't stay any longer
without becoming involved and moved, and that he
wanted to leave before this happened. I said, "Jeff,
why are you going to leave before you become
moved?" He replied, "Because if I am moved and feel
close to people, I will no longer be able to do the things
I do to people as a manager, and if I don't do the things
I do to people to manipulate, dominate, and control
them I won't be able to survive in the corporate
world." (By the way, he didn't leave.)

While this is a popular belief, it represents an impoverished model of business reality. It is this model that
earns for business its bad name and produces the
antagonism and apathy that is destroying the productivity of America.

You may find it difficult to accept, but conscious
love works in business too. Productivity and the happy
enjoyment of material well-being are a consequence of
us all transcending our imagined limitations to reveal
our inherent perfection and creative ability. This is the
purpose of conscious love.

Remember, conscious love does not happen by
chance.

Instinctual love exists as a function of our instincts
and is experienced whenever we are not dominated by
fear. What we popularly refer to as romantic, passionate love appears to happen by chance, but conscious
love does not happen randomly.

One of the most difficult lessons that conscious love
would have us learn is to be able to let go. Conscious
love knows how to let go. Letting go of what we love is
painful and in conflict with our instincts. Instinctual
love and conscious love are both pure. On the one
hand, instinctual love holds on and on; the other,
conscious love, knows when to let go.

It is a popular belief that the existence of real love

between two persons requires that their relationship be maintained in an active state forever, or at least "until death do us part." Though this may be a suitable model for the form of relationship we call marriage, it can be a devastating model when used outside this context.

Life is an educational adventure. Using education as a metaphor, let us consider the nature of the relationship between a student and a master. First, let us accept that there exists real love between the two, for such is often the case. Now let's ask ourselves, what is the symbol of success of such a relationship?

The answer is that the student graduates, i.e., the relationship is no longer maintained in its existing form. It is what we call "over." Conversely, if a relationship between a student and a master continues indefinitely it is usually a sign of failure, the interpretation being that the student has failed to achieve passing grades.

Consider this idea: Many of the relationships that you now consider failures may, in fact, have been successful graduations!

One of the consequences of our conscious love may be that the recipient discovers some measure of inherent perfection that you both now recognize needs further development elsewhere. Loyalty to the principle of conscious love demands that you support their going on in the world without you by their side. Members of the animal kingdom seem much better able to handle this than members of the human species. A mother bird always knows when her fledglings are ready to fly and empties them out of the nest when it is time.

Conscious love must sometimes know pain. As conscious lovers we must enroll ourselves in the process and be responsible for keeping ourselves enrolled in this process on a day-by-day basis. The outcome will always be a revelation of truth, beauty, and goodness.

This process requires of us the dedication and the discipline demanded by any true art form in which we seek mastery.

Conscious love is the most demanding art form we will ever come to know, and it offers the most powerful results. No other process can yield the experience of life we really want or allow for the existence of a world that we really want to live in.

Resolve to make conscious love the purpose of your life.